Technology Run Amok

Ian I. Mitroff

Technology Run Amok

Crisis Management in the Digital Age

palgrave
macmillan

Ian I. Mitroff
Professor Emeritus
University of Southern California
Los Angeles, CA, USA

ISBN 978-3-319-95740-1   ISBN 978-3-319-95741-8   (eBook)
https://doi.org/10.1007/978-3-319-95741-8

Library of Congress Control Number: 2018948652

Cover credit: Head & Phone Image © rudall30/Getty Images Security Camera Icon © Artdabana/Noun Project
Cover design by Tjaša Krivec

This Palgrave Macmillan imprint is published by the registered company Springer Nature Switzerland AG
The registered company address is: Gewerbestrasse 11, 6330 Cham, Switzerland

This book is dedicated to Donna Mitroff, my constant companion, best friend, and loving wife of 54 years. It would not have been possible without our daily conversations. They are a joy forever!

Preface

The Great Transformation/Revolution: The Triumph of Technology

The eminent British writer and scientist C. P. Snow said it best:

> Technology….is a queer thing; it brings you great gifts with one hand and it stabs you in the back with the other.

Nicholas Carr did as well:

> …More than two decades into the internet revolution, we now know that 'technology is an amplifier' for humanity's worst traits as well as our best. 'What it doesn't do is make us better people.'[1]

The enormous transformation for good and bad that is taking place all around us due to the unrelenting advance of technology and its unparalleled effects on our lives is the central topic of this book. It's nothing less than a revolution of monumental, if not cataclysmic, proportions. For many, it represents the clear triumph of technology over the human spirit.

This transformation qua revolution affects every aspect of our bodies and minds, the nature of communication, how we feel about and relate to others and ourselves, and not least of all, the meaning and structure of our basic institutions. Most important of all, it's altering the fundamental nature of reality itself. It's thus no exaggeration to say that the current transformation/revolution is among the greatest that humankind has ever experienced, if not the greatest.

This is not to deny in the least all of the positive benefits of technology. At its best, it's improved our lives in every way possible. We live longer and healthier lives because of technology, not to mention the greater ease with which we communicate and travel.

At the same time, there's no doubt whatsoever that the influence and impacts of technology are more pervasive and invasive than ever before. All of the incredible gadgets we've invented are not only transforming the world, but even more, they are reinventing and transforming us as well.

Unlike old-fashioned, bulky TVs, we not only carry today's technologies around with us everywhere we go—indeed, we're inseparably welded to them—but their demands are relentless. Not only have they disrupted our lives, but even worse, by constantly intruding and thus discouraging us from engaging in ordinary discourse and participation in civic affairs, they subvert normal democratic processes.

What makes the current transformation/revolution so different from others is that it's systemic. It affects every aspect of our being. Our lives have not only become deeply entangled with some of the most complex, messy systems ever created, but they have become literally synonymous them. For this reason alone, we need to have a far better understanding of the complex, messy systems that are affecting us in every way possible. This understanding is one of the primary aims of the book. My fervent hope is that it will allow us to gain a greater control of technology for the betterment of humankind.

In a word, the ethical management of technology needs to be given the highest priority. We cannot continue to dump the latest, great innovations and technologies on the world, and then afterward clean up their less than desirable effects. We have no choice but to do a far better job of thinking about, and thus mitigating, the negative aspects that accompany all technologies, especially before it's too late to do anything significant about them.

Time and time again, the history of technology shows that all technologies come with negative effects and consequences. More often than not, they are used in ways not envisioned by their creators. Not only are they abused, but they are misused in fundamental ways. Worst of all, far too many don't even want to think about the negative aspects of their prized creations. For instance, Facebook is one of the most prominent examples of our failure to anticipate the negative effects of social media on young people. Unfortunately, with its wanton display of horrific images, YouTube is just as bad, if not worse.

In brief, everything created by humans has unintended negative effects and undesirable consequences. This doesn't mean that we should thereby abandon the constant search for new and better technologies, but that we have to be constantly on-guard against the unintended negative effects and undesirable consequences of our wondrous creations. We have no choice but to do a much better job in anticipating and mitigating the ill effects and consequences that accompany all technologies.

To accomplish this, we not only need to have a far better understanding of the complex, messy systems that we're creating at an ever-increasing rate, but we need to put our knowledge into practice. In accordance with one of the prime tenets of the philosophical school known as Pragmatism, we don't really know something until we attempt to put what we think we know into practice to correct a series of problems that stimulated our search for knowledge in the first place. As an important aside, being "practical or pragmatic" as is the byword of many technologists is not the same as being philosophically reflective as Pragmatism constantly urges us to be.

Both the nature and the effects of technology cannot be understood apart from the complex, messy systems of which (1) they are fundamentally a part, (2) other systems with which they influence and interact, and (3) others that they are instrumental in bringing into being. In brief, understanding complex, messy systems is itself complex and messy. To further our understanding, I have drawn widely from such fields as argumentation, crisis management, nuclear strategy, psychoanalysis, philosophy, and Systems Thinking, to mention only a few.

Because I'm highly critical of the role that technology plays in contemporary society, I cannot emphasize enough that as someone with advanced degrees in engineering, I am anything but inherently hostile to it. Rather, I am extremely critical and highly skeptical of the mind-set of many technologists. In my view, they are not sufficiently aware of the serious crisis potential of their creations. They are neither inclined nor basically equipped to think about the negative social impacts of their inventions. And, of course, with so much money at stake, there are little incentives to dwell on, let alone contemplate seriously, the negative aspects and impacts. I am especially critical of the fact that never before have so few technology companies had the power to influence literally billions of people to their considerable advantage and profit.

In sum, this is not a simple book about simple ideas. While my intent is clearly to expand the thinking of readers so that we can all understand and cope better with technology, I have tried to make key concepts and ideas as accessible as possible. To accomplish this, I've used a wide variety of examples, many of which relate directly to technology as well as those that at first glance do not. Indeed, the later often illuminate important aspects of technology that the more obvious examples do not.

Crises of Unimaginable Proportions

One of the prime contentions of this book is that in addition to making our lives incomparably better in every conceivable way, the transformation/revolution we are undergoing threatens to bring crises of untold proportions. One cannot tinker with literally every aspect of our being and reality itself on scales not attempted before without producing major crises. In this sense, technology is now one of the greatest threats facing humankind. For this reason, a far greater understanding, and application, of crisis management is vital in coping with the crises brought about by our extreme dependence on—even worse, our deep addiction to—technology. I cannot stress enough that we cannot continue to dump the latest great technical innovations on the world and then later clean up their less than desirable effects. And, we cannot put the burden mainly on parents to monitor and protect their children from the harmful effects of technology, especially when they are up against some of the most powerful technology companies ever created. We have to do a far better job in anticipating the negative effects of our wondrous creations and doing everything in our power to mitigate their worst consequences.

However, before we can apply what we know from crisis management in dealing with the innumerable crises brought about by technology, we first have to understand as clearly as we can both the nature and the scope of the crises we face. Nevertheless, the crises cannot even be identified, let alone dealt with properly, independently of the complex, messy systems of which they are a part. Once again, we have no choice but to understand complex, messy systems far better than we have. As we shall see, this necessitates a substantial revision and expansion of previous ideas and knowledge about crisis management. It also requires a major revision of our thinking about systems. If we are truly to be able to see and deal with the potential crises facing us, then we have to involve a greater number and variety of factors that have been considered thus far in traditional discussions of Systems Thinking, and hence, crisis management.

For one, it requires that we understand the nature of paradox, for complex, messy systems are riddled through and through with fundamental paradoxes. For instance, bigger or more of something that is beneficial in the small is not always better in the large. Indeed, in many cases, Less is More. Hence, before we can manage them properly, we need to understand the paradoxes that plague complex, messy systems.

We also need to have a much better understanding of the psychological factors that are both basic parts of and impact complex, messy systems. In essence, they are infused with and impacted by powerful forces, many of which are beneath the level of consciousness. And once again, we need to surface and understand the fundamental belief system that undergirds our endless fascination and obsession with technology. I call it The Technological Mindset, a topic I explore in depth.

Previous Revolutions

Technology has always changed society in important, and in many, if not most cases, in unforeseen ways. For instance, the use of movable type to create the Guttenberg Bible not only changed what, but how we read. Most significant of all, it altered fundamentally how we interacted with our fellow beings.

Before Gutenberg, scribes painstakingly produced books one at a time. As a result, only the very rich and powerful institutions such as the Church could afford to have them. Since books were so rare, the few that were available were read aloud to small groups and audiences. In this way, books were an integral part of a long-standing oral culture where telling stories was not only the norm, but the principal way in which information was communicated. Stories were not only synonymous with information, but with knowledge itself. (Interestingly enough, with the advent of so-called social media, we've reverted to storytelling as the primary mode of communication and knowledge.) Thus, it's not surprising that the first printed books were also read aloud in small groups. Nonetheless, as they became less expensive, and thereby more widely available, over time people retreated to private spaces and became solitary readers—thereby continued the long line of separating and isolating us from our fellow man.

And of course, the first widely available books were strongly opposed by the clergy, for in effect they were displaced as the sole interpreters of the word of God. As we shall see, technologists have become the "new priests"—at very least, a "higher caste"—in that they not only play a fundamental role in the creation of new technologies, but a crucial role as their intermediaries.

Although the wide availability of books greatly impacted how we interacted with one another, they did not change the basic internal structure of our brains. With the advent of dime-store novels early in the twentieth century, there was considerable worry that they would harm the brains of impressionable young girls. New developments have always aroused fears and sparked resistance, often intense.

One of the things that's crucial about today's transformation/revolution is that current, not to mention future, technologies both promise and threaten to change the very structures of our minds, bodies, and social institutions—society itself—from top to bottom, from the outside-in, and the inside-out.

The Industrial Revolution

To take another, the Industrial Revolution did more than merely transform the meaning and the nature of work, which it undeniably did. It also did more than make transportation more efficient and speedier. It basically uprooted people from small villages in the countryside in which they lived side by side for centuries and forced them into dirty, dangerous, foul-smelling factories and even worse dwellings in cramped cities. For millions of people, it broke as never before the long-standing bond between humans and nature, and most of all, from one another.

In sum, the Industrial Revolution altered fundamentally our basic picture of the world. It was no longer a living organism governed by natural rhythms. Instead, it was a machine that was ruled other machines, most notably, rigid, unforgiving clocks that announced when it was time to rise, go to work, eat, and sleep. In essence, everything was nothing but a machine, although some such as humans and other animals were undeniably more complex than others.

A More Recent, Modern Invention

Consider a more recent, modern invention. There is no doubt that the advent of air conditioning in the twentieth century separated humans even further from one another. Before the widespread availability of air conditioning, on hot nights, people congregated on porches or steps in front of their houses. They not only conversed daily, but as a result, got to know one another. If not always for the better, they were intimately connected. (In a word, they were "connected" in ways far different from how Mark Zuckerberg conceives of it. They did not leave innumerable "posts," but instead spoke directly to one another.) Air conditioning changed all of this as people retreated to the relative comfort and isolation of their individual homes.

An Obligation to Learn from the Past

The objection is often made that no one could have foreseen all of the effects, both positive and negative, produced by previous revolutions. This is of course true to a degree. But this doesn't mean that we're not obligated to learn as much as we can from past efforts and mistakes so that we might better anticipate and avoid future ones. After all, we're supposed to be learning creatures par excellence.

The Current Tech Revolution

Learning from previous revolutions is made all the more important by the fact that nothing is like the current transformation/revolution we are undergoing. It both promises and threatens to alter every aspect of our being. It's already changed fundamentally how we communicate. Fewer and fewer of us, most notably young people, are brave enough to engage in unscripted conversations, one of the prime hallmarks of what it's meant to be human. For who knows what will occur in unpredictable circumstances? Do we dare risk offending anyone by not carefully planning what we'll text/tweet in 140 words or less?

In this regard, the results of recent studies in the UK are extremely disturbing.[2] They show unequivocally that social media are a serious threat to the mental health of young people. They only deepen feelings of inadequacy and anxiety. As a result, the UK is seriously considering passing laws that would restrict the content to which young people are exposed on the Internet, as well as apps for so-called smart phones.

In every way possible, the new transformation/revolution is not confined to the surface of our lives. It reaches to the very depth of our brains, bodies, in short, what's left of our souls. Even more, the threat to replace us with robots that can do everything quicker, cheaper, and more efficiently than humans can or want to do is all-too-real. To say that this is making a whole new slew of crises more likely, widespread, costlier, and deadlier is putting it mildly. For instance, how will society cope with the millions who make their current living by driving cars and trucks if they are replaced by driverless vehicles? Giving people a guaranteed income is not the answer since robbing people of work deprives them of their basic sense of dignity and purpose.

The point is often made that driving is both dirty and dangerous, and that therefore freeing people from it by utilizing better technology will be a boon to humankind. While I might agree with this in the long run, transitioning to driverless cars and trucks without offering people good replacement jobs is precisely one of the societal crises with which I'm concerned.

The Technological Mindset

This book not only examines the nature of the transformation we are undergoing, but most of all, it surfaces and critiques the underlying state of mind that is responsible for the revolution that is changing everything like nothing before it. Again, I call it The Technological Mindset. Examining it is a task of the upmost importance. Indeed, it's mainly responsible for the crises that are the direct result of our extreme dependence on, and even worse, our unbridled addiction to, technology.

Although it differs in key respects, The Technological Mindset bears a very close resemblance to what's been previously called Technological Utopianism. Nonetheless, The Technological Mindset is not merely an updated version of Technological Utopianism. It not only reaffirms earlier components, but it adds new ones as well. To repeat, the reach of technology is not only more pervasive—indeed, inescapably so—but more deeply invasive as well. For this reason alone, it constitutes a major threat facing humankind.

The key tenet of Technological Utopianism is: Technology is not only the solution to all our problems, but it's absolutely essential for human progress. This is aided by the firm belief that everything about technology is positive. As such, it must be strongly protected from any and all interferences from outside forces. Were it not for the heightened dangers that such beliefs pose, they would be little more than naïve. The key point is that The Technological Mindset is even more ominous.

I am especially critical of the notion espoused by many that, as we always have on previous occasions, we will somehow find ways to adapt to technology. Why should humans always be the ones to adapt to technology rather than the other way around? Does technology occupy such sacred ground that humans must every time adjust to it instead of it adjusting to us? What's the point of technology if it's not to serve humans and make our lives better?

I also take strong issue with the division of the world into Techno-Optimists versus Techno-Pessimists. Such a division is far too simplistic. I'm both and neither. If anything, I'm a Techno-Realist.

Closing Remarks

The great transformation/revolution we are experiencing is the result of the confluence of several major factors that have come together at this particular point and time in history. The first is not only the unrelenting pace of the development of new technologies, but their sheer numbers, pervasiveness, and invasiveness. The second is the underlying state of mind—The Technological Mindset—that is the driving force behind the unparalleled explosion of technology. A third is the underlying culture of startups and the predominantly male attitudes that they embody, namely a general lack of social maturity and the accompanying attitude of little if any concern with the societal impacts of technology. It therefore comes as no surprise that there is a marked inability and unwillingness to consider the negative consequences of one's prized creations.

It also comes as no surprise that serious concerns with the social responsibilities of businesses are essentially missing from the vocabulary of too many technologists. The unwillingness to consider negative consequences and the lack of concern with social responsibility are two of the prime components of "The Technological Mindset". Unfortunately, unless one considers the negative along with the positive, there is little hope of mitigating the worst of their effects.

Finally, while this is primarily a book about the tremendous impacts of technology on our lives, it's also fundamentally about the connections between technology and the larger society. Technology neither exists nor operates in a social vacuum. Indeed, it can't exist independently of all the human institutions that both nurture and sustain it. To reiterate an earlier point, while I have tried in every instance to use examples that pertain directly to technology, I've also used many that relate to much broader concerns. In many cases, they better illustrate the main points of the book. Nonetheless, as we shall see, all of the examples do relate to technology in important ways.

In sum, this book is not only about *Technology Run Amok*, but a world that is increasingly out of control as well. It's about the interdependencies between technology and society, human concerns in the broadest sense of the term.

Berkeley, USA   Ian I. Mitroff

Notes

1. Nicholas Carr, "Connection Can Bred Contempt," cited in *The Week*, May 5, 2017, p. 16.
2. "Facebook and Twitter Harm Young People's Mental Health," https://www.theguardian.com/society/2017/may/19/popular-social-media-sites-harm-young-peoples-mental-health.

Acknowledgements

I wish to thank Myles Thompson for his helpful comments on earlier drafts of the book.

Let me also thank Dr. Maureen Franey for the many fruitful conversations we've had concerning the broad applicability of the ideas of Melanie Klein to society as a whole, and not just to individuals for whom the ideas were originally developed.

David Ing and Susu Nousala helped with the many invaluable discussions we've had concerning wicked messes.

Lastly, I want to acknowledge Murat Can Alpaslan for his numerous contributions to my thinking over the years.

Contents

List of Figures

1

Introduction

Make no mistake about it. The unauthorized release of the private data of millions of Facebook users is not only the worst in its checkered history, but it's even worse for the tech industry as a whole. At the root of the crisis is a highly disturbing pattern. Unless this pattern is recognized for what it is, and ultimately curbed, then we'll just lurch from one crisis to another.

Indeed, in his testimony before Congress in April 2018, Facebook founder and CEO Mark Zuckerberg said that the crisis was due to his and the company's failure to see the "big picture." Although I deal with it throughout, this book is not primarily about Facebook. It's about a larger pattern that the crisis reveals about the tech industry in general.

Five components are key. Each is not only critical in its own right, but acting together, they spell disaster. They're guaranteed to bring an organization and its leaders to their demise. Although I discuss each in turn, in reality they operate in tandem. I also explore them in depth throughout:

© The Author(s) 2019
I. I. Mitroff, *Technology Run Amok*,
https://doi.org/10.1007/978-3-319-95741-8_1

1. Too much early success is actually detrimental to long-term survival and prosperity. It makes one complacent and thereby blind to the fact that there are serious problems lurking within one's basic business model that need to be addressed sooner rather than later.
2. The fact that one has weathered early crises also blinds one to the fact that one needs to start building a serious program in crisis management in order to be prepared for major crises later on that can't be easily dismissed.
3. The smug assumption that compared to technology, management is easy, if not trivial, prevents one from taking management seriously. I explore this later in terms of the phenomenon known as Splitting. It's responsible for dividing the world sharply into "good" versus "bad guys." It's the basis for demonizing those we hold in contempt.
4. The best crisis-prepared companies take immediate responsibility for their crises. They don't issue meaningless apologies that only make the initial crises worse.
5. And, finally, The Technological Mindset blinds its proponents to the fact that all technologies are abused and misused in ways not envisioned by their creators. Worst, it seriously hampers one from considering that all technologies come with serious downsides, and therefore, from taking appropriate preventative actions to mitigate their worst effects.

The Problems with Too Much Early Success

If a company is too successful from the start, e.g., its technology performs as intended and thus fulfills and even exceeds expectations, it breeds the mistaken belief that it will last forever. The bigger the initial success, and the longer it lasts, the greater the feeling that one has found "the golden goose that lays the legendary golden egg." In short, the founder/company have found the magic formula for success that should not be tampered with in any way.

In the case of Facebook, early success allowed it to coast longer than it should have on a faulty business model. In a recent PBS Newshour interview, Sheryl Sandberg, Facebook's Chief Operating Officer, said as much. From the very beginning, Facebook collected personal data from its users, which it then sold it to third parties for profit without any serious repercussions. Indeed, it hoodwinked customers into parting with their personal data with the overly simplistic slogan and promise of "being connected with the world."

The moral: beware of early success for it blinds one to future problems. Indeed, why think about problems when one is such a great success from the beginning?

The eminent professor and business consultant Peter Drucker captured it best of all when he called the phenomenon "the failure of success." Nothing fails more than quick and easy success.

The Problem with Weathering One's Initial Problems

Nonetheless, along with its early success, problems soon appeared. Cyberbullying was among the first of Facebook's problems to garner serious attention. So was the growing evidence that the more young people used it, the more depressed, isolated, lonely, and insecure they felt. In brief, they couldn't live up to all of the idealized portraits of others with which they were constantly bombarded.

Paradoxically, because Facebook weathered its initial early crises, it wrongly took it as sign that it didn't need to prepare for future ones that were not easily handled. The situation was made worse by the fact that it weathered even more serious crises such as its being used a platform by foreign governments to spread dis- and misinformation, and worse, hate speech. This only strengthened the feeling that it didn't need a serious program in crisis management that would have helped prepare it for future much more severe and devastating crises. The fact that it was used—more accurately, abused and misused—in ways that were not intended should have alerted it to the fact that it was a sitting duck for more serious abuses lurking in its initial business model.

Thus, Facebook and tech companies were not prepared for the havoc that resulted when a truly serious crisis that couldn't be ignored finally occurred. The fact that the personal information of over 50 million—which was later revised upward to 87 million—of Facebook users was used without their knowledge and permission not only resulted in a backlash against the company, but tech companies in general. The backlash was in fact so great that it caused a significant drop in the value of tech stocks not only affecting the market as a whole, but as well many more millions of people who were not users of Facebook.

Management Is Easy!

In addition, other less visible factors were also lurking in Facebook's largely taken-for-granted belief system. Unfortunately, it's an integral part of the tech community as well. It's nothing less than the smug assumption that compared to technology, management is easy, if not trivial.

When I went to engineering school some years ago (I have a BS, MS, and PhD in engineering, all from UC Berkeley), it was common to divide the world into "hard" versus "soft" subjects. Science and engineering were "hard," not just because they were difficult to learn and master, but because fundamentally they involved "objective, verifiable knowledge about the physical world, i.e., 'hard indisputable facts.'" In contrast, because they were riddled through and through with "subjective unverifiable judgments and opinions," the humanities and social sciences were irrefutably "soft." It followed that what they had to teach was mostly obvious and trite so one didn't need to waste one's time studying them.

Chief among the "soft subjects" was management. After all, how difficult was it to manage an organization? Once the objectives were stated—"make x amount of dollars by time y"—then people either got on board or you got others who would. This of course assumed that one's objectives were clearly known from the start and not changing and evolving, which they constantly are.

Sadly, far too many engineers and scientists are naïve at best when it comes to the social world. It's never just about making x dollars by time y, but of not causing irreparable harm to the most vulnerable members of society, and of course the environment. It also ignores the fact that one of the most difficult and important tasks of management is not only getting the buy-in of employees, but retaining them.

Although we've made some progress, prevailing attitudes are still largely the same. Management is "easy and soft," and technology is "hard in every sense and all important."

No wonder Facebook and the other tech companies don't take crisis management seriously and plan ahead for the worst. First of all, they really don't understand what crisis management is. It's not about being reactive and issuing platitudinous apologies after the fact. Truly effective crisis management is proactive. It not only consists of "thinking the unthinkable," but being prepared for it so that one knows what steps to take to limit damage and assume rightful responsibility when the worst occurs.

What the Best Crisis-Prepared Organizations Do and What the Unprepared Fail to Do

The best crisis-prepared organizations not only admit their mistakes immediately, but indicate clearly that they are prepared to take decisive steps to lower the chances of future mishaps. More often than not, it involves deep changes in a company's business model, leadership, structure, and culture. Without this, all the platitudinous apologies in the world only make the original crisis worse. For this and other reasons that I explore, I don't believe that Mark Zuckerberg is the right person to head a major organization. He obviously has the requisite skills to invent an important technology, but not the maturity and social skills that are necessary to manage a complex organization. Some have even called for even more drastic steps such as it's time for Facebook to go out of business entirely and be superseded by a new kind of social media company that is socially responsible from day one.[1]

Second, true crisis management is not a preparing for a single crisis, but being prepared for a whole range—a system—of crises. As one of the field's principal founders, and thus having worked in it for over

36 years, my colleagues and I have found repeatedly that no crisis is ever a single crisis. Instead, every crisis typically sets off a chain reaction of other crises.

Thus, Facebook's breach of the personal data of millions of users by Cambridge Analytica was not only the result of its flawed business model of selling data to third parties for profit, but it triggered a cascade of other crises. First, the initial crisis damaged almost irreparably Facebook's brand. How could one trust Facebook ever again? And, trust is the cornerstone of any business. Without it, no business can survive let alone prosper.

If this weren't bad enough, Facebook sent a shock wave throughout the entire tech world. Clear calls for government oversight and regulation to protect against the downsides of technology, including privacy breaches, were sounded as never before. This rattled the stock market, causing not only the value of Facebook's stock to drop substantially, but all tech stocks thereby causing the market as a whole to tumble, thereby affecting everyone.

In her recent interview on PBS, Sheryl Sandberg confirmed that Facebook stumbled from crisis to crisis without thinking about the big picture and thus preparing systemically for a whole range of crises. It merely reacted to each individual crisis as if it was isolated and independent of others. There was no prior thinking and preparation for a range of crises, certainly not the fact that any single crisis could set off a chain reaction of others, and thus, certainly not that all crises are interconnected.

The Pervasive Ill Effects of the Technological Mindset

Finally, one of the biggest reasons why technologists and tech companies are both unable and unwilling to contemplate the negative aspects and harmful consequences of their marvelous creations is that they are the prisoners of an even deeper taken-for-granted belief system that directs them to see only the positive aspects of technology. Indeed, they overly rhapsodize the positive aspects of their wondrous inventions to the near, if not total, exclusion of anything negative. This tendency is in fact one of the prime components of their underlying belief system, i.e., that technologists need only concern themselves with the positive aspects of their creations. Indeed, they should not waste their time thinking about anything negative. Leave that to others.

Once again, I call it The Technological Mindset. Until we acknowledge and deal with it, we will continue to suffer the ill effects of technology.

To counteract it, I propose that before any new technology is unleashed, a serious audit of its social impacts, both negative and positive, needs to be conducted by panels made up of technologists, parents, social scientists, teachers, children, etc. A technology should be adopted if and only if it continues to pass the most severe Social Impact Assessments we can muster. Social Impact Assessments are thereby the direct counterpart to Environmental Impact Assessments.

In short, the burden is placed squarely on technologists to justify their creations and to ensure that the negative impacts are not only given serious thought, but to the best of our efforts under control. Further, such assessments cannot be left to voluntary compliance. They have to be made mandatory. To help ensure this, I believe that a government agency akin to the FDA needs to be created and empowered to conduct Social Impact Assessments.

In this regard, the UK has taken the clear lead. They now require that the privacy statements that the users of social media and other technologies sign be stated in plain, easy to understand English. If they are not, then they won't be allowed to operate in the UK.

Ideally, as early on as possible, such assessments would be an integral part of the development of every new technology. Their cost would thereby be part of the total development costs. If history is any guide, as costly as they may be, they are far less than those associated with cleaning up after a major crisis. Indeed, the field of crisis management has shown repeatedly that those organizations that are prepared for crises not only experience fewer of them, but are substantially more profitable. In a word, they pick up potential problems before they turn into uncontrolled crises. Social Impact Assessments are not only the right ethical things to do, but they are good for business and society as a whole.

One of the key components of The Technological Mindset is the unbridled assertion that technology is the solution to all our problems, including those caused by technology itself. As a result, any/all damage and disruption to humankind are justified. If substantial numbers of people are inconvenienced, and worse, lose their jobs, then that's just the cost of progress. For the advance of technology is inevitable. What's more, the sooner we're all replaced by robots who can do everything cheaper and faster, supposedly the better off we'll all be, that is, for those of us who are still around to serve the robots. Humans are thus devalued as never before.

Contrary to the proponents of The Technological Mindset, the unrestrained advance of technology is not inevitable. In fact, a strong set of counter beliefs is needed so that technology can truly serve the betterment of humankind. For instance, another prime belief is that technology is the single most important factor responsible for material and economic progress. Without constant technological innovation, there can be no material and economic prosperity, period!

The counter is: No one seriously disputes the fact that technology is an extremely important factor in human affairs. But without appropriate social institutions both to nurture and to support it, technology cannot even exist, let alone contribute to material and economic progress. Contributing to the total well-being of society is even more of a challenge.

Concluding Remarks

In short, we need to change direction. Unless the underlying belief system driving technology is confronted, and ultimately changed, then nothing substantially will be altered. Technology will just lurch from one crisis to the next. Once again, Facebook has only added to the growing backlash against technology as a whole.

The time to embrace a different attitude to technology is now.

Note

1. Tim Wu, "Don'tFix Facebook. Replace It," *The New York Times*, Thursday, April 5, 2018, p. A25.

2

The Revolution of Everything

The crises that are a consequence of The Technological Mindset impact human society in a multitude of ways. The following are not only prime examples of the revolution we are in, but even more important, they illustrate the kinds of crises that are its direct result. In short, each shows the kinds of threats to basic values and dignity posed by various technologies, and most of all, with our basic obsession with technology in general.

Losing Our Minds by Transplanting Our Heads?

An article in *The Atlantic Monthly* sums up one of the most grotesque, if not bizarre, sides of contemporary science and technology.[1] A few— very few, thank God—medical scientists are seriously contemplating head transplants as a way to allow those whose bodies have been damaged beyond all hope of repair to continue living. As radical as this is, it's not enough to satisfy the Italian neurosurgeon Sergio Canavero who wants to go even further. He's promoting head transplants as "a step toward radical life extension for all human beings." There you have it,

© The Author(s) 2019
I. I. Mitroff, *Technology Run Amok*,
https://doi.org/10.1007/978-3-319-95741-8_2

one of science and technology's oft-stated goals: the complete control of nature. For humans, this means nothing less than immortality, the defeat of death altogether.

Never mind that even if it could be done successfully—for there are innumerable, daunting technical problems that would need to be overcome—transplanting a human head onto another human body would result in an entirely different person altogether. The plain fact of the matter is that the body is not just a "sophisticated carrying case for the brain." The brain–body organism is a very complicated, tightly bound system that is anything but the sum of its so-called separate parts. Instead, it's the product of a multitude of highly intricate interactions taking within a very complex system that is constantly changing.

> Sam Keen, the author of the article in The Atlantic, and someone who has written widely on neuroscience, put it as follows:

> …the brain has a hardwired internal representation of the [entire] body—a mental scaffold that resists radical change…[the person who] wakes up from [a head transplant] surgery…could well experience an agonizing, full-body phantom [like people who report feelings in an amputated limb].[2]

To put it differently, the revolution has broken down completely long-standing dualisms such as the mind versus the body. The mind cannot be separated from the total mind/body system, period!

While admittedly bizarre, the example is important for it takes to its logical (illogical?) end conclusion the often-expressed goal of science and technology to remake the entire world to our specifications, and thus put it completely under our control. Merely of conceiving of such a proposal, let alone seriously proposing it, is testimony to the times in which we live where technology plays an all-important role. Indeed, the goal of complete control over nature is one of the important aims of The Technological Mindset.

In his book, Homo Deus: A Brief History of Tomorrow,[3] Yuval Noah Harari takes the conquering of death to a whole new level, one that in my judgment is clearly beyond the pale of human decency. According to Harari, death is merely a "technical problem to be fixed and thereby overcome." There is no mention or regard for death as a profound human experience with deep cultural, emotional, and religious significance that brings people together to share their grief, mourn, and celebrate a person's life. No, all that is to be said is that like any other technical matter, death is just an important problem to be solved. To put it mildly, Harari's proposition is one of the biggest examples of denial writ large.

The reduction of one of life's most important and meaningful experiences to the cold language of technology not only demeans it, but assaults and diminishes our humanity. It's a deep insult to the values we place on life by not acknowledging death as one of the most meaningful and intense of all human experiences.

But then, one of the prime components of The Technological Mindset is that technology is the solution to all of our problems, including the problems caused by technology itself!

Improving a Part Does not Necessarily Improve the Whole

With the best of intentions, doctors are continually working to improve the health of young prepubescent girls. To achieve their desired goal, they've promoted major changes in diets that have been shown to make substantial improvements in health. However, such advances do not come without major costs. Improved diets have led young girls to develop much earlier sexually. This in turn has led to earlier sexual experiences, often with unfortunate consequences.

It's not that health via diets should not be improved, but that one cannot tamper with just one part of a complex biological/social system without affecting it in countless ways that are not always intended, let alone desirable. The inability, worse yet, the unwillingness, to anticipate the undesirable along with the desirable is one of the greatest shortcomings of our age, if not of all ages. While this has always been true, the major unintended, negative side effects are more immediate and extensive than ever. In the particular case at hand, we seriously perturb the basic value of letting young girls develop normally.

Note that while it's highly tempting to construe the example as merely one of "teenage sexuality," to do so misses an important point. It's more to do about our intervening in complex systems without our having given serious thought to probable unintended consequences.

Always Connected

> Forget smartphone and watches. DuoSkin, a new product from Microsoft and the MIT Media Lab, can turn your epidermis into a touch pad. Or a remote. Made with naturally conductive gold leaf, DuoSkin places a technology interface directly on your body… The process is designed so people can customize both form and function for a tattoo that lasts only a day. The goal, says lead designer Cindy Hsin-Liu Kao, is to create technology that's as personal as lotion or makeup, so 'it really blends into the wearer's identity.'[4]

In an extremely important book that deserves to be read by every parent of young children and teenagers, ALONE TOGETHER: Why We Expect MORE from TECHNOLOGY and LESS from EACH OTHER (Basic Books, 2011), MIT Professor Sherry Turkle documents repeatedly how Facebook coupled to smart phones is a serious threat to healthy child development. Facebook and cell phones prey upon children and young adults 24/7 like nothing before them. The scores of children and young adults that Turkle interviewed over the course of many years report that contrary to expectations—and especially the hype—Facebook did not help them to "truly connect" with one another, certainly not in the ways that child development experts would have them. It only added to their growing sense of deep isolation, loneliness, and estrangement from one another. If anything, Facebook leads to an overly obsessive preoccupation with the constant presentation of a carefully orchestrated and fragile self. In brief, the pressures for presenting a perfect image to the world are truly overwhelming. The result is that Facebook and other social media platforms are as highly addictive as any powerful drug.[5]

An episode of 60 minutes only adds to the need for being wary. It featured a former Google employee who left the company precisely because he was tired of fighting a losing battle against the proliferation of apps that were explicitly designed to hook users, i.e., to feed their addiction to their innumerable devices. In other words, the attachment of young people to their devices is not left to chance. Instead, it's deliberately orchestrated.

One of the saddest, most dire consequences of instant texting is that it's impaired the ability of young people to engage in open-ended conversations. They don't want to engage in them because there are no clear-cut rules for (a) their initiation, (b) keeping them going smoothly as they unfold, and (c) especially ending them without offending the other party. It's become far easier to engage in filtered, impersonal "texts" than in face-to-face unscripted, unpredictable conversations.

According to Turkle, all of this is further compounded by the fact that many parents are not available emotionally and often not physically as well. Many parents are so stressed by their jobs and constantly on call such that they have no time for themselves, let alone their children. In saying this, Turkle is not blaming parents per se. Rather, if she is placing blame, she is putting it squarely on the social demands of jobs and modern living conditions in general.[6]

One has to be an extreme optimist—a Techno Optimist—to believe that more technology is going to solve the problem of overly stressed parents. But then, The Technological Mindset believes that there is a technical solution to every problem.

More often than not, everyone is on their cell phones at the dinner table, if they even get together for meals anymore. We are not merely tethered to our cell phones, but they have truly become integral parts of us. When it comes to smart phones, we've already become cyborgs. The quote above on gold leafs that are applied to our skins and function like smart devices is testimony to the fact that engineers have already developed technologies by which we can seamlessly control our devices (us?)

merely by touching the skin on our arms.[7] We have become the screens by which we communicate, if that's what we really do anymore.

It's not bad enough that the sleep patterns of young people have already been seriously disrupted by means of placing their cell phones directly under their pillows lest they miss an important text/tweet during the night. Now their skins will be buzzing all night long as well. Technology thereby disrupts the value of uninterrupted sleep that is essential for normal functioning, not to mention development.

The few families that have broken the tyranny of emails and texting have imposed a strict rule of no cell phones or devices whatsoever at the dinner table. Conversations are the norm. But this takes enormous courage to break the habit of incessant texting. They also try to curb the feeling that cell phones must be on all night long lest someone miss an important text or email.

One of the major contentions of this book is that *before **any** new technology is unleashed, a serious audit of its social impacts, both negative and positive, needs to be conducted by panels made up of technologists, parents, social scientists, teachers, children, etc.* Indeed, the need for continuous, ongoing audits of all technologies, no matter where they are in their lifecycles, is one of the chief lessons of crisis management. If only for the reason that technologists are generally resistant to social audits, if they are even aware of them to begin with, we cannot leave them to voluntary compliance. They have to be made mandatory. This is one of the prime conclusions from my lifelong work in crisis management.

For instance, before Facebook was unleashed, there are good reasons to believe that teams of parents, kids, psychologists, historians of technology, etc., would have come up with the serious possibility of its being used as a major means of cyberbullying and thus have suggested ways of curbing it. The pressure on social media companies to look out for the welfare of users needs to be constant and unremitting. Time and again, it's clear that they will not do anything responsible without constant and considerable social pressure.

Facebook's allowing the use of ads featuring anti-Semitic slurs—not to mention its most recent crisis of the unwarranted release of the private information of up to 87 million of its users—only adds to the need for regulating technology companies, something that they resist strongly.

They are like earlier industries that fought any and all regulations until their own ill behavior forced it upon themselves. There are no valid reasons why as part of an orchestrated program of crisis management, Facebook couldn't have envisioned this and other crises for which it should have been prepared.

Make no mistake about it. Those technologies whose negative effects are dangerous, irreversible, and unpreventable need to be strictly controlled, if not banned altogether. The plain fact of the matter is that there are no technologies without significant negative effects. The only issue is whether we have enough sense of moral and social responsibility to do something seriously about them before they do irreparable harm.

In this regard, Common Sense Media has pioneered "Sleeping Bags for cell phones"—dedicated pouches where one can place one's devices—for the purpose of taking time-outs from texting at the dinner table and at bedtime. The supreme question of course is, "Why wasn't this conceived of and initiated from the very beginning?" It would have been one of the best examples of proactive crisis management, heading off a crisis before it began. It's precisely because no one can predict with perfect certainty all of the consequences—positive and negative—of any technology that continuous, ongoing crisis audits need to be a fundamental, and thereby a regular, part of its ongoing management.

The innumerable devices that young children constantly use take a substantial toll on their emotional development. In a series of experiments, children who spent five days at a camp where no devices were allowed were compared to a carefully matched group of children who were not at the camp and thus used their devices freely during the same time period. At the end of their stay, the children who spent five days at the camp were significantly better in identifying a broad range of emotions when presented with pictures of people than those who had continually used their devices.[8] For this and other reasons, I worry about what a lifetime of exposure does to our ability to relate appropriately to others.

Finally, Facebook has been accused of helping brands target teens who feel worthless.[9] Facebook has not only used image-recognition tools to collect the emotions of its users, but it's sold the information to third parties who then use it to target vulnerable teenagers. Such behavior is beyond reprehensible. It shows the utter lack of ethics and responsibility of those who direct social media. It goes directly against the basic value of protecting young children from harm.

Should There Be an App for Everything?

"…a new project…seeks to modernize how we deal with trash by making our bins smarter and…more social…The bin's inside lid is equipped with a tiny smartphone that snaps a photo every time someone closes it…in order to document what exactly you have thrown away. A team… then evaluates each photo. What is the total number of items in the picture? How many of them are recyclable? How many are food items? After this data is [sic] attached to the photo, it's uploaded to the bin owner's Facebook account, where it can be shared with other users. Once such bins are installed in multiple households, BinCam creators hope, Facebook can be used to turn recycling into a game-like exciting competition. A weekly score is calculated for each bin, and as the amounts of food waste and recyclable materials decrease, households earn gold bars and leaves. Whoever wins the most bars and tree leaves wins. Mission accomplished: Planet saved!

Nowhere in the academic paper that accompanies…BinCam…do the researchers raise any doubts about the ethics of their undoubtedly well-meaning project. Should we get one set of citizens to do the right thing by getting another set of citizens to spy on them?…Could the 'goodness' of one's environmental behavior be accurately quantified with tree leaves and gold bars? …Will participants stop doing the right thing if their Facebook friends are no longer watching?"[10]

BinCam may be a humorous example of technology run amok, but it literally pales in comparison with other "innovations" like Zamzee and Fatworld that essentially turn controlling obesity into a game. Weightier still are apps that monitor blood pressure, temperature, and blood oxygenation levels. What happens if such personal data are turned over to insurance companies and potential employers? What happens if we don't just have external apps that are on our devices, but instead, medical chips and implants that are integral parts of our bodies? On the positive side, such data could prove invaluable to one's personal physician in monitoring health. On the negative, it could be used against one in applying for insurance, jobs, etc. Given the large-scale breaches of personal data that are more and more common, what's to ensure the privacy of one's personal health data?

Recently, Elon Musk has proposed directly implanting electrodes in our brains in order to enhance and improve cognitive functions. The ultimate dream is to allow us to upload and download our thoughts more efficiently so that we'll be better able to compete with Artificial Intelligence (AI). It could also be used to treat numerous health conditions. Needless to say, little if any thought has been given to the fact that this will hasten our becoming cyborgs, plus all of the unintended side effects such as hacking into our brains.

Should there be an app for everything? My response is a firm "NO!" At least not without knowing who and what will control the app and how it will be used, and more onerous still, how it will be abused.

Once again, I cannot stress enough that *before **any** new technology is unleashed, a serious audit of its social impacts, both negative and positive, needs to be conducted by panels that are made up of technologists, parents, socials scientists, teachers, children, etc.* They need to be part of regular ongoing crisis audits. Those that pose serious harm need to be controlled, if not banned altogether.

A Threat to Basic Values

These are only a few of the many examples that are indicative of the transformation/revolution we are undergoing. We shall encounter more as we proceed. But one thing should be clear from our brief review of the impacts of technology. They not only challenge but threaten some of most cherished values: privacy, well-being, not to being taken advantage of by unscrupulous companies, in short, to be respected and treated with dignity.

Notes

1. Sam Kean, "The Audacious Plan to Save This Man's Life by Transplanting Head and What Would Happen If It Actually Works," *The Atlantic Monthly*, September 2016, pp. 51–58.
2. Kean, op. cit., p. 57.
3. Yuval Noah Harari, *Homo Deus: A Brief History of Tomorrow*, Harper, New York, 2017.
4. Julia Zorthuan, "Big Idea, 'Smart' Tatoos," *Time*, September 5, 2016, p. 19.
5. For a more extensive treatment of the addictive aspects of technology, see Stephanie Brown, *Speed: Facing Our Addiction to Fast and Faster—And Overcoming Our Fear of Slowing Down*, Berkeley, New York, 2014.
6. See also, Brown, ibid.
7. Zorthuan, op. cit.
8. Y. T. Uhis, et al., "Five Days at Outdoor Education Camp Without Screens Improves Preteen Skills with Nonverbal Emotion Cues," *Computers in Human Behavior*, Vol. 39, pp. 387–392.
9. Paul Armstrong, "Facebook Is Helping Brands Target Teens Who Feel 'Worthless,'" *Forbes*, May 1, 2017.
10. Evegeny Morozov, *To Save Everything, Click Here: The Folly of Technological Solutionism*. Public Affairs, New York, 2013, p. 2.

3

It's All About Systems

When future generations look back, they will criticize us soundly for our repeated failures to think and to act systemically. Systems Thinking is critical, for as we shall see, it's the underlying basis of crisis management. If we are to have any reasonable chance of anticipating and thus mitigating the crises that are due to our uncritical acceptance of technologies good and bad, then we need to embrace crisis management far more than we have to date. For this reason alone, we need to examine how and what it means to think and to act systemically. At the end of the chapter, I present two novel ways of achieving it.

First, we need to clarify what is and what's not a system. If something has one and only one part, then it's not a system. To take an extremely simple, if not trivial, example, although it's the result of multiple manufacturing and distribution systems, by itself, a pencil is not a system. It only becomes part of a system when a person uses it to satisfy some intended purpose, writing to a friend, relative, or co-worker, etc. In somewhat different terms, inanimate, mechanical objects such as pencils have functions, but only humans—including other animals—engage in purposive behavior and thus have purposes. As a matter of fact, humans

© The Author(s) 2019
I. I. Mitroff, *Technology Run Amok*,
https://doi.org/10.1007/978-3-319-95741-8_3

deliberately create objects with specified functions, e.g., cars, in order to satisfy intended purposes such as efficient means of transportation.

In short, a system has at least two parts. Furthermore, I contend that something is a system *if and only if* it not only has at least one technical part, but in addition, it has at least one part that is human/social.

Further, as I make clear shortly, the common, taken-for-granted notion that a system is nothing but a bunch of boxes and variables with arrows indicating all the interactions between them is at best only half of the story. A system is much more than just boxes, variables, and arrows. First of all, we rarely know all the boxes and variables, let the full range of interactions between them.

Consider again the example in the last chapter about improving the diets of young girls and thereby their health. The good doctors who wanted to improve the health of young girls were in all likelihood not thinking systemically, or doing so only in a very limited sense. They assumed implicitly that the problem that they and young girls faced was essentially bounded and well structured. It was bounded in that it was a problem that involved nutrition and nothing else. It was well structured in that supposedly the measurable improvement in one variable, the composition of diets, led unequivocally to measurable improvements in another variable, health. In other words, they thought they knew what the major variables were and their interactions.

Unbeknownst to them—at the very least, unacknowledged by them—the doctors were one of the most important parts of the system that they were hoping with the best of intentions of improving. Their limited conception of the system was one of the most important factors in the system's resultant behavior, the unintended effects on the sexual behavior of young girls. Merely by describing a system, not only are we intervening in it, but we are thereby one of its most critical parts!

The kinds of problems we face are increasingly unbounded and unstructured, if not ill-structured (An unstructured problem is one that does not automatically come with a clear definition or formulation, e.g., a single well-defined structure. Thus, different stakeholders are highly likely to formulate and hence structure the problem differently. Ill-structured problems seriously resist any attempts at defining and hence structuring them.). Thus, the health of young girls cannot be isolated from the larger issues occurring in society as a whole. Young people live in a society where they are literally constantly bombarded with messages extolling sex and sexual permissiveness. It's a world of sexting and widely available pornography. It's a world that it is constantly shaped by social media and per-pressure. As a result, the problem is anything but simple, bounded, and well structured. And, this is only one example.

As we shall see in the next chapter, the problem has only gotten worse with the advent of even more complex and messy systems. It's a world where traditional education organized primarily around solving bounded, well-structured problems—essentially overly defined exercises—drawn largely from separate, supposedly autonomous disciplines not only breaks down completely, but becomes as a result an even bigger part of the problems we are facing.

Finally, the BinCam example shows that ethics is a part of every system that is of interest to humans. As a matter of fact, every one of the examples in Chapter 2 not only concerns systems, most of which we are unaware, but most importantly, ethics.

Argumentation as a System

Since this book deals with numerous arguments, I want to discuss a very special method for analyzing and treating arguments that shows that they naturally form a system. It is in fact one of the most important examples and methods of Systems Thinking.

The distinguished historian and philosopher of science, Stephen E. Toulmin proposed the following important schema for analyzing and appraising arguments.[1] Every argument terminates in a Claim. The Claim is the end result or conclusion of an argument. It basically asserts that such and such is the case, e.g., that humans are primarily responsible for global warming. Claims also assert that we ought to undertake such and such series of actions in order to eliminate problems, e.g., we need to curb drastically our use of fossil fuels.

In order to reach, and thereby ground the Claim, every argument makes use of Evidence and a Warrant. Typically, the Evidence is broader than brute facts alone, for it includes "reasonable suppositions" in addition to "hard facts." Thus, in the case of global warming, the Evidence is not only the results of innumerable scientific studies that establish that humans are primarily responsible for global warming, but also the "fact" that 97% of "reputable scientists worldwide" are in strong agreement with the Claim.

The Warrant is the "because" part of an argument. If the Evidence is true, or highly plausible, and further, if the Evidence implies the Claim, then the "process of implication" is the Warrant. In the strongest possible case, the Claim follows directly from the Evidence because the Evidence is the direct cause of the Claim. That is, if the items in the Evidence occur, then the Claim follows automatically. In either case, the Warrant is the bridge between the Evidence and the Claim. The Warrant allows one to go from a limited set of Evidence to a more general proposition, the Claim.

In the case of global warming, the Warrant is the proposition that after all other sources, such as natural variations in the Earth's temperature fluctuations, are eliminated, then humans emerge as the major source of global warming. Notice that in many cases it's difficult to separate the Evidence and the Warrant completely.

Toulmin also introduced two other key features of arguments: the Rebuttal and the Backing. The Rebuttal consists of all the challenges, direct and indirect, to the Claim, Warrant, and the Evidence. Thus, the Evidence and Warrant both can be faulty, incomplete, or not strong enough, and thus, not support the Claim. In addition, the Claim can be dubious altogether and thereby not accepted on its face value.

If the Warrant is not accepted on its own, then the Backing is the deeper set of reasons why the Claim follows from the Evidence. In my terms, the Backing is the general set of background assumptions and/or conditions that are necessary to support the Evidence, Warrant, and Claim, e.g., the expertise and credibility of climate scientists who presumably have followed accepted scientific procedures necessary to establish that humans are primarily responsible for global warming.

The important point is that taken together, the Claim, Warrant, Evidence, Rebuttal, and Backing form a highly interrelated system. What one concludes from the overall conjunction of the Claim, etc., depends on what one assigns to the plausibility of each of the elements. Although I shall not always mention it explicitly by name, I make use of the Toulmin Argumentation Framework (TAF) throughout.

The Myers-Briggs: A Psycho-Social Method of Systems Analysis

For years, my colleagues and I have used a special interpretation of the Myers-Briggs Personality Test as a method of systems analysis. Although originally developed to analyze the personalities of individuals, we've used in ways such that it not only applies to, but illuminates aspects of systems that other forms of analysis do not always reveal. Besides, one of the key principles of Systems Thinking is that the methods and frameworks developed for individuals apply equally to each and any level of systems, and vice versa. Thus, as much as individuals, organizations and societies also have "personalities," etc.

The Myers-Briggs Personality Test is based on the influential work and thinking of the eminent Swiss psychoanalyst Carl Jung. As a highly educated European of his time, Jung was extremely well versed in history, literature, philosophy, and psychology, to mention only a few of the fields in which he was knowledgeable. Jung noticed repeatedly that the same fundamental differences in outlook emerged time and again no matter what the particular subject matter he studied. As a result, he was able to extract and thus codify the differences into a few basic personality dimensions. Isabel Myers-Briggs and her daughter eventually constructed a test based on Jung's dimensions so that one could easily assess a person's personality.

Two main dimensions of the Myers-Briggs Personality Type Indicator—really the Jungian system—are important for our purposes: one, what one considers valid data or information on which to base one's decisions, and two, one's preferred method of analyzing data in order to reach a decision. The first dimension is bounded at each end by one of two different ways of securing what one regards as valid data/information or Evidence: Sensing (S) versus Intuition (N). The second is bounded by two different ways of analyzing one's preferred data/information in order to reach a decision: Thinking (T) versus Feeling (F). In effect, T and F embody two different kinds of Warrants. Combining the two dimensions in all possible ways results in four very different and distinct "personality types": Sensing Thinking (ST), Intuitive Thinking (NT), Intuitive Feeling (NF), and Sensing Feeling (SF) (Note that the letter N is used for Intuition since the letter I is already used for Introversion, an important dimension, but one that is not relevant for our purposes.).

Sensing (S) "types" instinctively approach any situation and break it down into its "natural independent parts." They then proceed to collect "hard data and facts" about each of the parts.

Intuitive (N) "types" instinctively approach any situation and look for the "connections and interactions" between the so-called individual parts. In other words, N types are systemic in their outlook.

It cannot be stressed enough that no single outlook is inherently better than or superior to the others. The various outlooks are merely different. They not only need one another to keep themselves honest, but they are fundamentally dependent on all of the others in order to work, even though they rarely realize it and hence often have extreme difficulty in acknowledging it.

Thinking (T) "types" prefer to analyze any situation by means of impersonal analytic techniques such as Logic, Statistical Analyses, etc. Feeling (F) "types" prefer to approach any situation in terms of their personal likes and dislikes, e.g., how they feel about a person or situation, etc.

In terms of technology, STs are most often concerned with "hard data" about the market potential of any proposed technology. For instance, what are the prospects that a technology will be a big winner financially? They are also concerned with "hard facts" about the detailed technical properties about any proposed invention, what it will do, potential hurdles that need to be overcome before it can be brought successfully to market, etc.

NTs are primarily concerned with whether any proposed technology will be original and markedly innovative such that it will totally disrupt accepted ways of thinking. Thus, Uber intentionally disrupted the taxi industry (And, Uber's toxic culture has ended up disrupting itself. Uber is thereby a prime example of the failure to think and to act systemically.).

NFs are concerned about whether any proposed technology will help and/or harm the most vulnerable members of their community. They are especially concerned with how technologies can be abused. They are thus concerned with the broader social impacts and implications of all technologies.

SFs are concerned with how any technology will make their personal lives and that of their immediate families and friends better or worse. They are thus concerned with immediate social impacts.

As an important aside, NTs and NFs are most likely to be concerned with multiple definitions and meanings of the "vulnerable members" of a community. STs and SFs are most likely to zero on a single definition that they regard as "final."

Ideally, each of these attitudes ought to work together for they not only affect one another in countless ways, but they are interdependent. None of them can really work without addressing the concerns and issues of the others. For instance, without their always acknowledging it, STs presuppose a stable society, i.e., NF, without which ST cannot even exist, let alone work. And, NFs presuppose STs in order to get a society to function day-to-day.

Although we shall not always refer explicitly to the Myers-Briggs, it will always be there in the background.

Concluding Remarks

In the pages and chapters to follow, we shall see that The Technological Mindset is based primarily, if not exclusively, on ST. It also has important aspects of NT as well. It poses a threat to humanity because it contains virtually no reference to the elements of NF and SF, two of the prime set of attitudes and beliefs that make us human.

Note

1. Stephen E. Toulmin, *The Use of Argument*, Cambridge University Press, New York, 1958.

4

Wicked Messes: The Pioneering Work of Horst Rittel and Russ Ackoff

Thomas Friedman, the eminent columnist for *The New York Times*, has stated well the point of this chapter. I quote:

> The days of clear-cut, satisfying victories overseas, like opening up China or tearing down the Berlin wall are over. U.S. foreign policy now is all about containing disorder and messes. It is the exact opposite of running a beauty pageant. There's no winner, and each contestant is uglier than the last.[1]

One of the most pressing problems facing humankind is coping with the complex, messy systems—and in many cases, just plain messes—that we've created, both intentionally and unintentionally. Not only do they impact every aspect of our lives, but in many cases, they pose major threats to our very existence. Global warming and ISIS, which I discuss shortly, are just two of the many pertinent examples.

I want to talk about the most complex messy systems of all—wicked messes. To do this, we first need to talk about wicked problems. We

---

Portion of Chapters Four through Nine appeared previously as blogs in The Huffington Post.

© The Author(s) 2019
I. I. Mitroff, *Technology Run Amok*,
https://doi.org/10.1007/978-3-319-95741-8_4

then need to talk about messes. Wicked messes are the conjunction of the two. As we shall see, The Technological Mindset is one of the thorniest wicked messes of all. This is one of the major reasons why technology is so difficult to tackle, let alone control.

Even though they are obviously ongoing and thus constantly in flux, I discuss global warming and ISIS. The reason is that they are prime examples of wicked messes. By definition, not only are they difficult to deal with them, but such difficulties are in fact one of the major properties of wicked messes.

Wicked Problems

In 1973, in a classic essay, "Dilemmas in a General Theory of Planning," Horst Rittel and Mel Webber introduced the concept of wicked problems.[2] Rittel and Webber argued that social problems were fundamentally different from problems in engineering and the physical sciences. In a word, problems in the social and policy sciences, public policy in general, were the complete opposite of "tame problems."

Even though they didn't use the same terms in describing them, by "tame," Rittlel and Webber meant that a problem was essentially both bounded and well structured. Bounded problems are in essence not only distinct, but limited and confined. One can "rope 'tame problems' off" and consider them independently of one another. Thus, in modeling bounded problems, other problems don't have to be considered. In addition, they are bounded in another important way. They generally involve only a few variables.

For example, in computing the distance D that a 5-pound weight falls, one doesn't need to take into account the material out of which the weight is made, or whether other weights are in its immediate vicinity, or at least one doesn't have to do so in introductory physics classes where one learns the formula, $D = 1/2\ G\ T^2$, where G is the acceleration due to gravity (approximately 32 feet per second squared) and T is the time in seconds that a weight falls. Thus, the problem is well bounded in that only a few variables are involved. Applying the formula, one finds that a 5-pound weight falls approximately 64 feet in 2 seconds.

"Well structured" means that a problem can be encapsulated in a relatively simple physical model that can be expressed mathematically; as a result, it often has a neat mathematical solution. The formula for the distance D that a weight falls in T seconds, $D = 1/2 \, G \, T^2$, is a prime example.

In sharp contrast, wicked problems have none of the supposedly desirable properties of tame problems. First, they are unbounded. They can't be isolated and separated from the host of other problems to which they are intimately connected. Thus, problems of climate change, crime, employment, homelessness, housing, and income inequality are neither separate nor distinct. So-called solutions, assuming that they exist, for one problem, not only affect, but are dependent on solutions to the others. (See the example at the end of this chapter.) And, they involve many variables, many of which are unknown, and worse yet, unknowable.

Wicked problems are also "wickedly ill-structured." No single discipline or profession has a monopoly or final say on how they are to be represented and thus modeled, if they can be at all.

For another, wicked problems don't stay solved, assuming once again that there are solutions to them in the first place. Even if it exists, a solution for one time and place is not necessarily a solution for other times and places, certainly not for all political and social actors, stakeholders in the widest possible sense of the term.

If this weren't bad enough, so-called solutions to wicked problems are more likely than not to give rise to other even worse problems. Thus, "solutions" become new "problems." For instance, while necessary in many situations, aggressive policing has played a significant role in an epidemic of the shooting and resultant loss of lives of unarmed black teenagers and young men. This has in turn resulted in huge, and sometimes violent, protests against police departments, and the severe loss of trust in the communities that police serve, and without which they cannot do their jobs.

Messes

In 1979, in a highly critical speech—"The Future of Operational Research Is Past"—that he gave to the Operations Research Society of America, of which he was one of the early founders and past presidents, Russ Ackoff appropriated the word "mess" to stand for a whole system of problems that were so highly interconnected such that no individual problem could be taken out of the mess and studied on its own independently of the entire mess of which it was a part.[3] To take any of the so-called individual problems out of the mess, and to consider it separately, was to distort irreparably both the nature of the problem and the entire mess. In short, problems don't exist independently of all the other problems to which they are connected.

As Ackoff put it:

> …Managers are not confronted with problems that are independent of each other, but with dynamic situations that consist of complex systems of changing problems that interact with each other. I call such situations messes. Problems are abstractions extracted from messes by analysis; they are to messes as atoms are to tables and chairs. We experience messes, tables, and chairs; not problems and atoms.
>
> Because messes are systems of problems, the sum of the optimal solutions to each component problem taken separately is not an optimal solution to the mess. The behavior of a mess depends more on how the solutions to its parts interact than on how they act independently of each other.[4]

In his typical, pithy manner, Ackoff put it best: "Managers don't solve problems; they manage messes."

In brief, we don't live in the nice neat world of mathematically precise, well-formulated technical problems, if we ever really did. We live in a world of ever-growing and more complicated messes. Increasingly, we live in a world of wicked messes. Thus, to put it mildly, death is not merely a "technical problem to be solved," but part and parcel of a wicked mess with deep emotional and social meaning!

The ISIS Mess

The ISIS Mess is one of the wickedest wicked messes of all. Worse still, it's not only pathological, but it's cancerous. As such, it's one of the best examples of a wicked mess. As Phyllis Bennis has noted:

> "The US war against ISIS, President Obama's iteration of George Bush's much-heralded and long-failed 'global war of terror,' presents [a...] complex set of paradoxes and contradictions: The US is fighting against ISIS alongside Iran and the Iranian-backed Baghdad government in Iraq, and fighting in Syria against ISIS alongside (sort of) the Iranian-backed and US opposed government in Damascus. And all the while, the US and its Arab Gulf allies are arming and paying a host of largely unaccountable, predominantly Sunni militias that are fighting against the Syrian government and fighting—sort of—against ISIS. Meanwhile, in Iraq, the Iranian government is arming and training a host of largely unaccountable, predominantly Shi'a militias that are fighting against ISIS and –sort of—alongside the US backed Iraqi government.
>   It's a mess."[5]

Although it was written a few years ago, an article in *The Atlantic Monthly*, "The Hell After ISIS," still provides some of the most powerful insights into The ISIS Mess, and thereby more generally, into wicked messes. Indeed, the article cuts straight to the heart of the mess. The author, Anand Gopal, has "been meeting with Sunnis from western Iraq in order to understand how the war against ISIS looked to members of the largest group still living in ISIS's self-declared caliphate...They have found themselves caught between the Islamic State on one side and U.S.-allied forces—the Iraqi government, its army, and Shiite militias—on the other. In this telling, the anti-ISIS forces are just as violent as the entity they are fighting."[6]

> Many Sunnis in Anbar resented that the U.S. intervention not only benefitted certain tribes over others, but also produced a Shia-dominated government. After the Americans withdrew in December 2011, the Islamic State of Iraq and other insurgent groups sought to deepen these divides

through a campaign of violence targeting Shiite civilian progovernment [sic] tribal sheikhs. In 2012, nearly 400 car bombs went off nationwide.[7]

The result is that the term "wicked" hardily begins to describe The ISIS Mess. It's more akin to a "pathological, if not a cancerous disease." One of the basic, characteristic properties of such messes is that every action that is undertaken to improve them is virtually guaranteed to do the opposite: create as much harm as good. In somewhat different words, every seemingly positive action has the high potential of producing dangerously harmful interactions with each and every part of the mess. As the quotes from Phyllis Bennis and Anand Gopal illustrate, enemies become friends, and friends are enemies. It's a complete topsy-turvy world. And of course, the U.S. bombing in Syria due to the use of deadly gasses by the Bashar al-Assad regime on civilians is just part of the mess, and in this sense, furthers it.

The situation is directly akin to cancer where the body's bad cells attack the good ones. Thus, under the guise of helping those who are besieged by ISIS, those who are the recipients of U.S. aid become worse off. The result is that what's a "good cell" and what's a "bad cell" (or equally, "good" versus "bad" actions) are in extreme doubt, if they can even be clearly distinguished or separated from one another. In short, what's "good" and what's "bad" are highly contentious, as they always are. I discuss this important aspect of wicked messes further in the next chapter.

As a consequence, a previous heuristic[8] that I formulated for coping with messes—"examine a mess for the most improbable interactions between the parts, for if they hook up, they have the potential for producing a major crisis"—takes on a whole new meaning. (One only has heuristics or approximate rules of thumb for coping with messes because once again they are not well-structured exercises with nice, neat bounded solutions. In other words, they do not result in exact, fixed, and stable solutions. As a result, there are no clear-cut algorithms for defining, let alone coping with messes.) In a cancerous mess, the heuristic now becomes: "the most unlikely parts of a mess <u>will not only hook up</u>, but <u>definitively cause</u> major crises." Indeed, <u>every part</u> of mess will hook in unexpected ways to cause a myriad of crises that can only be described as "cancerous." Crises are thereby some of the most prominent and important aspects of wicked messes, where once again, the term "wicked" is often too mild a term.

The preceding represents more than the commonly understood notion of "unintended consequences," which of course it is. The notion of "unintended consequences" is taken to a whole new level, or bottom as it were. There is no part of a cancerous mess that is not subject to "unintended consequences." This above all makes such messes unmanageable at the present time. Every action that is undertaken in the hope of making them more manageable has a high probability of making them less manageable. In pithy terms, More Leads to Less, which is the topic of another chapter.

As is so often the case, one is left with military interventions as the last, if not only, hope of subduing as best one can an organized group, i.e., ISIS, with whom one can't engage in anything even approaching rational negotiations. The supreme question is who should lead such military forces. The debate is between those who believe fervently that as a world leader, the USA has to be in command in assembling and leading a coalition to wage war against ISIS. Others believe just as fervently that ISIS wants nothing more than to see the USA get bogged down in another war in the Middle East that it can't possibly win. As a result, acrimonious ethical and moral debates are fundamental parts of wicked messes.

Here's precisely where another interaction rears its head. Wanting to ban all Muslins from entering the USA as President Trump proposed doesn't help in enlisting their aid in identifying radical elements or in building coalitions with Arab states.

Finally, there are strong indications that the U.S. coalition is winning the military war against ISIS. However, as Anand Gopal has reported, given that considerable backlash is brewing against the USA with regard to how it's treated some of the Sunni tribes, The ISIS Mess may be a classic case of winning the war, but losing the mess!

Nonetheless, like everything having to do with the ISIS Mess, the proposition that we are winning militarily is itself highly contentious. Writing in *Foreign Affairs*, Hal Brands and Peter Feaver put the matter as follows:

None of the four [major] strategies [for containing, let alone defeating ISIS] is ideal. The extreme options—disengagement and surge—promise to dramatically reduce the threat. But both would likely fail in costly ways, and both are politically untenable today. The middle choices pose less risk and are more politically palatable. But they also promise far less and would likely leave the United States stuck in a protracted conflict.

[President] Trump must therefore pick the best of a bad lot. Despite his campaign rhetoric, the least worst choice would be an approach close to the medium-footprint strategy used to defeat ISIS today: an aggressive campaign encompassing air strikes, drone attacks, special operations raids, and small deployments of regular ground troops in response to specific threats, all in support of regional partners. This approach is imperfect, and it will not achieve decisive victory in a conflict that shows few signs of ending soon. But it is the most likely way of delivering an acceptable degree of security at an acceptable price.[9]

Notice carefully the two heuristics that are embedded in the quote above with respect to picking a strategy for fighting ISIS: one, "pick the best of a bad lot, i.e., the least worst," and two, pick "the most likely way of delivering an acceptable degree of security at an acceptable price." In this way, the heuristics for dealing with a mess are some of its most important parts! Unlike simple exercises, the strategies for defining the elements of wicked messes and for coping with them are parts of the mess! Nothing is independent of a mess.

It's a mess!

The World Mess

Finally, consider how all of the following messes are linked together. It shows that very different kinds of thinking are required to make sense of complex messy systems. In short, different messes are part of a gigantic wicked mess, The World Mess, perhaps the largest mess of all:

The Sustainability Mess cannot be tackled without tackling
The Global Warming/Climate Change Mess, which cannot be tackled without tackling

The Renewable Energy Mess, which cannot be tackled without tackling
The Middle East Mess, which cannot be tackled without tackling
The Terrorism and Weapons of Mass Destruction Messes, which cannot
be tackled without tackling
The Fundamentalism and Corruption Messes, which cannot be tackled
without tackling
The Poverty Mess, which cannot be tackled without tackling
The Crime Mess, which cannot be tackled without tackling
The Racism Mess, which cannot be tackled without tackling
The Education Mess, which cannot be tackled without tackling
The Income Distribution Gap Mess, which cannot be tackled without
tackling
The Unemployment Mess, which cannot be tackled without tackling
The Global Financial Mess, which cannot be tackled without tackling
The European Union Mess, which cannot be tackled without tackling
The Aging Population Mess, which cannot be tackled without tackling
The Social Security Mess, which cannot be tackled without tackling
The Health Care Mess, which cannot be tackled without tackling
The Washington Political Mess, which cannot be tackled without
tackling
The Media (failure of the fourth estate) Mess, which cannot be tackled
without tackling
The Capitalism Mess, which cannot be tackled without tackling
The Sustainability Mess.

Thus, the whole cycle of messes repeats itself endlessly, that is, until we learn how to deal appropriately with messes.

Concluding Remarks

Consider briefly how each of the Myers-Briggs personality types deals with messes. STs (Sensing Thinking) instinctively focus on the elements for which they feel standardized methods of analysis and research are best equipped to handle.

NTs (Intuitive Thinking) focus on the major interactions between the various "components" but only after looking at the whole of a mess.

NFs (Intuitive Feeling) focus on how their communities will be impacted by a mess.

And, SFs (Sensing Feeling) focus on how they personally will be affected.

Notes

1. Thomas L. Friedman, "Trump's 'Miss' Universe," *The New York Times*, Wednesday, May 11, 2016, p. A23.
2. Horst W. J. Rittel and Melvin M. Webber, "Dilemmas in a General Theory of Planning," *Policy Sciences*, Vol. 4 (1973), pp. 155–169.
3. Russell L. Ackoff, "The Future of Operational Research is Past," *The Journal of the Operational Research Society*, Vol. 30, No. 2 (February 1979), pp. 93–104.
4. Ackoff, op. cit., pp. 99–100.
5. Phyllis Bennis, *Understanding ISIS and the New Global War on Terror*, Olive Branch Press, Northhampton, MA, p. 1.
6. Anand Gopal, "The Hell After ISIS," *The Atlantic Monthly*, May 2016, p. 81.
7. Gopal, op. cit., p. 82.
8. See Ian I. Mitroff, Lindan B. Hill, and Can M. Alpaslan, *Rethinking the Education Mess: A Systems Approach to Education Reform*, Palgrave Macmillan, New York, 2013.
9. Hal Brands and Peter Feaver, "Trump and Terrorism," *Foreign Affairs*, March/April 2017, p. 28.

5

The Psychodynamics of Messes: The Pioneering Work of Melanie Klein and Donald Winicott

Melanie Klein is rightly regarded as one of the giants of psychoanalysis. Her ideas are especially pertinent with respect to wicked messes, although one would barely know it, for they are never discussed in conjunction with systems, let alone wicked messes.

Psychoanalytic thinking is important because a great deal of the components of every system not only relate to individuals and society, but because many are below the plane of consciousness. As a result, one is not conscious of all of the elements that comprise a system, let alone of all their interactions. Recall that in the case of diets and young girls, much of the intense pressure to confirm due to peer behavior is unconscious.

Portion of Chapters Four through Nine appeared previously as blogs in The Huffington Post.

© The Author(s) 2019
I. I. Mitroff, *Technology Run Amok*,
https://doi.org/10.1007/978-3-319-95741-8_5

Splitting

Klein's ideas are indispensable in understanding the important phenomenon known as Splitting. Indeed, she is generally credited with having discovered it.

Splitting is important because it's responsible for the sharp division of the world into "'good' versus 'bad' guys." Needless to say, Splitting was a major component in the 2016 campaigns of all the Republican candidates as well as those of Senator Sanders and Secretary Clinton. More generally, because wicked messes involve a large number of actors—stakeholders in the broadest sense of the term—Splitting is virtually guaranteed to be present. Virtually, all messes of any degree split the world sharply into "good" versus "bad guys or forces." Recall in the case of The ISIS Mess that who's and what's good versus bad is constantly in flux depending on the particular context or situation. Further, Splitting is one of the most prominent features of President Trump's Administration.

As we shall see, the division of the world into "hard" versus "soft" subjects is one of the most pertinent, contemporary examples of Splitting as it applies to technology.

Splitting is also a major factor in how the various Myers-Briggs personality types view one another. Thus, STs and NTs often see NFs and SFs as hopelessly emotional, whereas NFs and SFs see STs and NTs as cold and mechanical, totally devoid of human feelings. As a result, they regularly demonize one another.

The Good and the Bad Mother

By means of play therapy, which she literally invented, Klein was able to get at the earliest, preverbal, unconscious fantasies of children during the first two to three years of their lives.

Play therapy involves observing carefully how children play with toy figures representing the various members of their families and other important characters in their lives. For instance, are the toy figures angry and rough with one another? Which ones are favored versus tossed aside? The therapist is thereby given a window into what's going in the lives of children, their families, friends, etc.

The point is: If Freud discovered the child in the adult, then Klein discovered the infant in the child. She thus pushed back even further our understanding of the roots of human behavior.

Via play therapy, one of Klein's earliest discoveries was that the fantasies of very young children revealed that there is an extremely powerful and destructive side to humans during the first years of their lives. Their fantasies were basically due to the fact that very young children experienced extreme anger and frustration over the fact that they didn't have complete control over the primary caretaker who was responsible for feeding them both physically and emotionally. Indeed, very young children literally experience the issue of control as a matter of life and death. The need for complete control is not only one of the earliest, but most primitive defense mechanisms available to humans for protecting themselves against the extreme anxiety brought about by an uncertain and unpredictable world.

When Klein wrote early in the twentieth century, the main caretaker was primarily the mother. Fathers did not share as much then as they do now in caring for young children.

Klein established that under the age of two or so, children universally split the image of the mother into a "good mother," who cared for and administered to the child's every need exactly when the child wanted it, and a "bad mother," who had to discipline the child and couldn't be there exactly when the child demanded it. Because the child's mind was not yet mature enough, it couldn't comprehend, let alone accept, that the "good mother" and the "bad mother" were one and the same. To the young child, there were two separate and distinct mothers.

This helps to explain why historically fairytales have had such a tremendous appeal to children worldwide. The "good witch" and "bad witch" help young children cope psychologically with the issues they are struggling to comprehend. Namely, they cannot accept and thus reconcile that the good mother and the bad mother are one and the same. Fairytales thus allow children to "act out" safely the emotional conflicts they are experiencing. That's precisely why the "bad witch" is always killed—indeed has to die—and the "good witch" always triumphs.

This also helps to explain what's involved in the breach of trust, and why it's felt so deeply. A person's first sense of trust is not only established by, but imbued with all of the pleasant feelings associated with the "good caretaker." Conversely, the breach of trust is associated with the "bad caretaker." No wonder why any person or institution that betrays our trust stirs up deep feelings. Thus, when Facebook allowed itself to be used as a vehicle for the dissemination of Fake News and salacious ads, it stirred up some of the deepest feelings that humans ever have. The final and irreparable blow was its role in the unauthorized release of the personal data of millions of users. It's nothing less than deep betrayal.

The Functions of Myths

Myths often serve much of the same function for adults as fairytales do for young children. Unfortunately, they often don't allow adults to act out safely their unconscious fantasies. In many cases, they magnify fears and anxieties, especially when they are the products of shared cultures that harbor bad feelings that have lasted for centuries. Fake News, which I discuss in more detail later, is just one of the latest examples of anxieties and fears run amok. Only in this case, it's aided and abetted by the latest technology.

Healthy Containers

One of the critical tasks of parents is to provide a "healthy container" to help the young child literally "contain" the raging emotions pulsing through them uncontrollably. (The notion of a "healthy container" is due to one of the other giants of child psychology, Donald Winicott.) If the parents do not either over- or underreact to the child's emotions, verbal outbursts, and fantasies, then the child eventually learns to contain his or her emotions and hence heal the split images between the "good" and the "bad" parents. The child eventually comes to accept both cerebrally and emotionally that the "good" and the "bad" aspects of the parents are located in the same person. He or she also eventually comes to accept that there are good and bad sides to everyone, especially themselves. Nonetheless, even under the best of circumstances, Splitting lasts a lifetime.

The Paranoid-Schizoid Position

Klein termed the earliest stage of human development "the Paranoid-Schizoid Position." It was "paranoid" because the young child was deathly afraid that the parent would either hurt or abandon him or her, and thus not meet the child's needs at all—"schizoid" because of the phenomenon of Splitting.

Most children naturally develop out of this earlier stage, but again, some form of Splitting and paranoia stay with us our entire lives. Thus, in times of extreme stress or threat, we shouldn't be surprised to find people regressing or reverting back to the Paranoid-Schizoid Position. For this reason, I was not surprised in the least that Splitting played a major role in the 2016 campaigns of the Republican candidates. With his constant denigration of blacks, Hispanics, women, Muslims, etc., it played a prominent role in President Trump's campaign. And most dangerous of all, as President, calling the press the "enemy of the people" is one of the worst examples of Splitting. It's exactly the type of language used by ruthless despots and dictators to demonize the opposition and silent the press.

Sadly, Splitting also played a major role in Senator Sanders' campaign as well with his constant, unrelenting attacks on Wall Street and his near inability to see anything positive in Capitalism.

In brief, both President Trump and Senator Sanders play handily to one of the primary fears associated with Splitting, i.e., the feeling that "_they_ are out to get us." This is not to say that there are not legitimate fears and things that deserve justifiable anger, but to deal with those that are legitimate, one first has to root out those that are the product of irrational, unconscious fears.

The Depressive Position

Klein also identified a subsequent, follow-on stage of human develop-ment that she termed the "Depressive Position." In this stage, the child finally accepts that the "good" and the "bad" mothers are one and the same. At least for the time being, the child moves beyond Splitting. Klein termed this stage "Depressive" because the child remembers and thus feels sad about his or her previous hostility toward its mother.

Above all, it's important to understand that all of this takes place unconsciously. One certainly cannot explain any of this to the unde-veloped minds of children. And, one cannot necessarily explain it as well to adults who are under the grips of Splitting. More than ever, we need friendly, nonthreatening adult figures who can provide desperately needed hope and reassurance that the world is not breaking asunder. If we do not, then the door is wide open for demagogues who not only prey upon our deepest fears, but magnify them for their own gain.

Splitting in Action

Hot-button issues are generally one of the best places to observe Splitting in action. They are generally characterized by:

1. Different parties have fundamentally different definitions of the basic issues at hand. It's not just that different parties have very different remedies and solutions, which they obviously do, but even more basic, they don't start with the same definitions of the basic issues or problems. Further, in framing their definitions, they don't use neu-tral terms. Typically, the language is highly inflammatory and volatile. (As we shall see, the use of extreme language is one of the main fea-tures of The Technological Mindset.) For instance, those who are in favor of early childhood vaccinations, and in giving a battery of shots all at once in a single session, see them as "helpers." Those who are staunchly opposed to vaccinations see them as "poisons." Splitting is thus a prominent feature of what's been termed "Vaccination Wars." Both sides constantly denigrate the other, often in the most vicious of terms.

2. Different parties have different perceptions of who and what's responsible for the problem or problems. Thus, those who are _not_ in favor of early childhood vaccinations see government, the medical establishment, and the big pharmaceutical companies (big Pharma) as "enemies." Those who are in favor see them as "protectors" and "friendly safeguards." Once again, Splitting is a prominent factor.

3. They differ with respect to who the guilty parties are, if any. For instance, even though it's long been discredited as a valid medical theory, many still believe that childhood vaccinations for measles, mumps, and rubella (MMR) cause autism. In a nutshell, big Pharma is responsible for autism and not parents who have been wrongly blamed for causing it due to poor parenting.

4. They differ with respect to whether the responsible parties are good, bad, innocent, evil, intelligent, stupid, trustworthy, etc. Once again, those who are opposed to early childhood vaccinations generally believe that the government, the medical establishment, and big Pharma can't be trusted. They act solely in their own self-interests instead of the public's whom they are supposed to serve.

5. They also differ with respect to who is an expert. For good and for bad, the Internet has enabled many to believe that they can look up their own facts with respect to complex, messy issues, come to their own conclusions, and thus be better informed than the so-called experts.[1]

In short, hot-button issues raise the most intense human emotions. That's precisely why they're "hot."

Management Is Easy and Soft While Technology Is Hard

One of the most egregious examples of Splitting pertains directly to technology. This is the situation that I referred to earlier in Chapter 1.

Recall that when I went to engineering school, it was common to divide the world into "hard" versus "soft" subjects. Science and engineering were "hard," not just because they were difficult to learn and master, but because fundamentally they involved "objective, verifiable knowledge about the physical world, i.e., 'hard indisputable facts.'" In contrast, because they were riddled through and through with "subjective unverifiable judgments and opinions," the humanities and social sciences were irrefutably "soft." It followed that what they had to teach was mostly obvious and trite so one didn't need to waste one's time studying them.

Chief among the "soft subjects" was management. After all, how difficult was it to manage an organization?

Although we've made some progress, prevailing attitudes are largely the same. Management is "easy and soft" and technology is "hard in every sense and all important."

No wonder Facebook and tech companies don't take crisis management seriously and plan ahead for the worst. First of all, they really don't understand what crisis management is. It's not about being reactive and issuing platitudinous apologies after the fact. Truly effective crisis management is proactive. It not only consists of "thinking the unthinkable," but being prepared for it so that one knows what steps to take to limit damage and assume rightful responsibility when the worst occurs.

Concluding Remarks

Unfortunately, as the world has become more complex and thus requires that at very minimum we acknowledge the existence of wicked messes, Splitting works to the contrary. Splitting allows one to retreat to the much simpler world of bounded, well-structured exercises. If anything, "bad forces" are responsible for complex, messy problems. In this way, blaming takes the place of true problem solving, i.e., coping with wicked messes.

The work of Melanie Klein not only shows why it's so difficult to bring people together that are deeply divided, but what's required to heal deep divisions. There must be enough people in responsible positions who are able to live with ambiguity. They must be both willing and able to acknowledge that there is good and bad in everyone, especially themselves. They must be willing and able to see and acknowledge that they and their opponents share something in common, indeed more than they'd like to admit. The movement from the Paranoid-Schizoid Position to the Depressive Position is one of the most difficult and crucial tasks facing humankind and societies as a whole everywhere.

Finally, the contentions that "old people and women can't do tech" are two of the most egregious examples of Splitting that pertain to tech.[2] Tech companies would do well to have a "senior executive in charge of guarding against Splitting!"

Postscript

Homo Deus,[3] to which I referred earlier, contains some of the most egregious examples of Splitting. Thus, humans are nothing but a collection of "organic algorithms" that control the firing of neurons in their brains. As such, humans are vastly inferior to "silicon-based algorithms." In the future, all humans will be useless and obsolete except for those few elite humans that have been "upgraded."

Notes

1. Tom Nichols, *The Death of Expertise: The Campaign Against Established Knowledge and Why It Matters*, Oxford University Press, New York, 2017.
2. Tad Friend, "Getting On, Why Ageism Never Gets Old," *The New Yorker*, November 20, 2017, pp. 46–51; Sheelah Kolhatkar, "The Disrupters," *The New Yorker*, November 20, 2017, pp. 52–63.
3. *Homo Deus*, op. cit.

6

Why Bigger Is Not Always Better, Further Thoughts on Complex, Messy Systems

Because of the continuing waves of mass shootings in this country, this chapter has been particularly painful to write. It's a sore testimony to both our inability and unwillingness to control a dangerous technology.

I begin by noting that what's true in the small generally breaks down in the large. This is another essential aspect of complex, messy systems. Bigger or more is not always better. This is certainly true in the case of young girls where by themselves better diets do not necessarily improve their overall well-being.

One of the most powerful ways of demonstrating this is by means of the especially bitter and contentious issue: the regulation of guns. The starting point is the fact that the USA has approximately 4% of the world's population, but 40–45% of the world's guns. If more guns were the answer, then the USA ought to be the safest nation on the planet, which it is not. In fact, other Western industrialized nations actually have more crime than we do, but because of the widespread availability of guns, ours is generally more lethal.

Portion of Chapters Four through Nine appeared previously as blogs in The Huffington Post.

© The Author(s) 2019
I. I. Mitroff, *Technology Run Amok*,
https://doi.org/10.1007/978-3-319-95741-8_6

To understand the nature of the paradoxes that are a fundamental part of wicked messes, consider the following.

A Fundamental Paradox

In the 1950s, at the height of the cold war, the USA and the Soviet Union realized that their huge nuclear arsenals gave rise to a fundamental paradox: They existed for the prime purpose of assuring that they would **_not_** be used.

To protect their missiles, both sides loaded them onto submarines that were capable of hiding indefinitely in the vast oceans of the world. We continue to do so to this very day. In this way, the side that was attacked first would always have enough missiles to retaliate and hence to destroy the other many times over. Since the situation was completely symmetrical, nuclear weapons existed for the prime purpose of assuring that neither side would use them to start a nuclear war that no one could win. This was enshrined in the doctrine of Mutually Assured Destruction, or MAD, an apt acronym if there ever was.

MAD Was Not the Only Paradox

Unfortunately, MAD was not the only paradox associated with nuclear weapons. As a result of my research, I discovered even more.

Both sides protected their land-based nuclear missiles by putting them in silos buried deep in the ground. Covering the silos with massive amounts of concrete offered further protection. More concrete led to greater or more felt security. In pithy terms, More Led to More.

But putting more concrete only encouraged both sides to load multiple warheads onto their missiles so they could more easily penetrate the silos. More concrete threatened the other side more and led to an arms race. Thus, More Led to Less. That is, More Led to Less Felt Security.

It occurred that less concrete would threaten one's adversary less and thus lead to greater felt security, i.e., Less Leads to More.

But, since it made no sense to have one's missiles protected by no concrete at all, less concrete led to less felt security, i.e., Less Led to Less.

More Leads to More and Less Leads to Less are the two primary modes of thinking that prevailed for hundreds, if not thousands, of years. If they were well supplied, trained, and led, an army with greater numbers of soldiers could generally defeat an army with fewer. But because of their enormous destructive power, nuclear weapons altered these long-standing tenets (really heuristics) of war. The side with more nukes was not necessarily superior to one with less. If just one or two nuclear weapons survived a first strike, then the side that was attacked first could still launch a severe counterattack that could harm irreparably the side that started a nuclear war.

The biggest paradox of all was due to the fact that the various strategies or paradoxes governing the use of nuclear weapons were constantly cycling through all four modes simultaneously: More Leads to More, More Leads to Less, Less Leads to More, and Less Leads to Less. They not only existed, but functioned simultaneously. Each gave rise to all of the others. As it were, they were locked into a never-ending, deadly dance.

Nuclear weapons were constantly cycling through all of four modes because the basic phenomenon was highly unstable. It was fundamentally unbounded and ill-structured.

Underlying all of them is the fact that at some point what's good in the small becomes bad in the large. Bigness or plenty turns back on itself.

To put it mildly, this is another factor that complicates coping with wicked messes. For example, in the case of The ISIS Mess, one constantly has to challenge whether helping one faction more than others is actually counterproductive in the sense that it makes things worse, i.e., More Leads to Less, that is, What's Seemly More or Better Leads to Less.

Guns

With these ideas in mind, let me return to the highly contentious issue of guns. To repeat, the USA has roughly 4% of the world's population, but 40–45% of the world's guns. Again, if more guns were the answer, then the USA ought be the safest planet on the globe, which it is not. The widespread availability of More Guns Has Led, among many things, to More Mass Shootings (i.e., Less). We are in the grips of a perverse form of MAD, i.e., its breakdown. More guns have not automatically led to fewer gun homicides.

Indeed, in the October 2017 issue of *Scientific American*, Melinda Wenner Moyer reviews the multitude of studies on the role that guns play in promoting versus curbing violence.[1] The results are unequivocal. Guns contribute greatly to suicides and homicides. Having a gun in one's home increases some three to seven times the chances of a suicide or homicide. Guns the things that are supposed to protect us become the things from which we need protection. No wonder why the states with lax gun laws experience more not less deaths due to guns. This is one of the most pernicious forms of More Leads to Less.

The one variable above all others that stands out in predicting mass shootings is the sheer numbers of guns in a society. The more guns there are, the greater the heightened chances of mass shootings.

Against this, rabid gun proponents argue that there are no limits to the benefits of guns, i.e., More Guns Indefinitely Lead to Greater Security. They also argue that More Regulations Lead to Less Safety, and thereby that Less Regulations Lead to Greater Safety, etc.

Technology

The same kinds of paradoxes are also at the root of our basic inability to control technology. Those who are its arch supporters are generally in favor of as few regulations with regard to technology as possible. In a word, they are under the grips of More Leads to More, i.e., more technology leads to more, if not unlimited, positive benefits. As a consequence, they are generally unable to foresee the problems, if any, which are associated with technology. More Leads to Less is not part of their basic mind-set.

In *The Death of Expertise: The Campaign Against Established Knowledge and Why It Matters*,[2] Tom Nichols makes the case forcefully that the Internet, which was supposed to be a major factor in promoting the spread of information and knowledge, has in fact led to exactly the opposite. It's a major factor in the spread of disinformation, and worst yet, misinformation. It's tricked people into believing that they're highly informed when in fact they're grossly misinformed.

As Nichols puts it:

> The Internet is the largest the largest anonymous medium in human history. The ability to argue from a distance, and the cheapened sense of equality it provides, is corroding trust and respect among all of us, experts and laypeople alike. Alone in front of the keyboard but awash in websites, newsletters, and online groups dedicated to confirming any and every idea, the Internet has politically and intellectually mired millions of Americans in their own biases. Social media outlets such as Facebook amplify this echo chamber...[3]

A World of Paradox

We live in a world where increasingly, every aspect and phenomenon are governed by paradox. This means not only recognizing the basic existence of paradox, but acting differently. For instance, More Leads to More, More Leads to Less, etc., apply with equal force to the global economy, in short, to any and everything that is messy and complex. The result is that increasingly, Less is More. But this also means very carefully reducing more of something presumed to be unequivocally good so that Less Leads to Less is under control.

Notes

1. Mellinda Wenner Moyer, "Journey to Gunland," *Scientific American*, October 2017, pp. 54–63.
2. Nichols, op. cit.
3. Nichols, op. cit., p. 132.

7

Big Data ≠ Big Wisdom: Mismanaging Twenty-First-Century Problems with Nineteenth-Century Thinking

There is no doubt whatsoever that technology greatly enhances, magnifies, and improves the senses—it allows us to hear and see things and act at distances that we can't without it—but it does not necessarily improve our sensibilities with regard to what's worth doing, hearing, and seeing in the first place. The Internet, especially so-called social media, often magnifies our worst impulses. They allow us to do and say things that hopefully one would not do and say in person. In this regard, they have contributed to the rise of rudeness in society as a whole. In short, technology, which allows to see and to travel farther and faster, etc., does not necessarily make us better informed, let alone wiser. It certainly does not tell us when to turn off our innumerable devices.

The thing that changed my sensibilities permanently is the fact that when I was studying for my PhD in engineering, I intentionally chose to take a 3 1/2-year minor in philosophy of science. Furthermore, the particular kind of philosophy of science that I studied was

Portion of Chapters Four through Nine appeared previously as blogs in The Huffington Post.

I. I. Mitroff, *Technology Run Amok*,
https://doi.org/10.1007/978-3-319-95741-8_7

fundamentally interdisciplinary. It stressed repeatedly that no single discipline or profession had a monopoly on the truth or the way to study reality. Unlike those versions of the philosophy of science that were dominated in the 1960s, it emphasized that the physical and social sciences were on an equal par. As a result, interdisciplinary inquiry is the only guarantor of which I know for minimizing Type Three Errors, solving the wrong problems precisely.

Expert Consensus

One of the primary ways for acquiring knowledge in Western societies is by means of Expert Consensus. In this system of inquiry, "truth" is that with which a reputable group of experts agrees strongly. Commonly, it is the average of a set of tightly bunched data, observations, scores, etc., that have been collected in accordance with the exacting standards of accepted scientific methodology.

Global warming is one of the most important examples of Expert Consensus. The body of reputable climate scientists worldwide is essentially in overwhelming agreement that human activities are mainly responsible for global warming. This "fact" which is based on innumerable scientific studies—and not on raw opinions—is taken as strong Evidence that the debate whether humans are or are not responsible for global warming is over even if all the mechanisms for it are not understood completely at the present.

Agreement is as important in science as it is in any field of human endeavor. In fact, one could argue that it is even more important because so much is riding on the outcome of scientific knowledge.

Big Data

The latest incarnation of Expert Consensus is Big Data. The hope is that by compiling enough data from different sources, it will reveal, say, the "underlying, true buying habits and preferences" of a selected group of consumers. However, writing in *The New York Times*, Alex Peysakhovich and Seth Stephens-Davidowitz note that for Big Data to actually work one is dependent on Small Data.[1] One needs old-fashioned interviews and surveys to understand in depth why people give the numerical responses they do. In other words, by themselves, numbers are never enough. A single number can never summarize completely how people feel about an issue that is of importance.

The biggest downfall of Expert Agreement is that it assumes that one can gather data, facts, and observations on an issue or phenomenon without having to presuppose any prior theory about the nature of what one is studying. It assumes that data, facts, and observations are theory and value-free. It's not just that one can't interpret anything without a theory of some kind, but even more basic, one can't collect any data in the first place without having presupposed some understanding and/or theory about the phenomenon that underlies the data, certainly why this particular set of data is important to collect and how they should be collected so that they accurately reflect the "true nature of phenomenon."

In contrast, the philosophical school known as Rationalism assumes that theories are free or independent of data, facts, and observations. In principle, the formulation of theories is dependent only upon pure thought or logic alone. In actuality, theories are dependent upon the background, experience, and life history of the person or persons formulating the theories.

In sum, I'm extremely critical of Big Data, not because the concept makes no sense at all, or that I'm fundamentally opposed to collecting data. Instead, as it's currently conceived, the concept is deeply flawed. If all data are dependent upon some underlying theory or theoretical concepts before the data can even be captured, let alone analyzed, then what does it mean to put all kinds of data indiscriminately into larger and larger pools?

Unless one knows a lot about the different theories that underlie different sets of data, and how they can be reconciled and integrated, then one is literally squishing together apples and oranges. Mush is the inevitable result, i.e., the crisis of Big Data.

Concluding Remarks

In <u>Homo Deus</u>,[2] Yuval Noah Harari elevates Big Data to the status of a religion! Indeed, he gives it the terrible name of "Dataism." One of the prime tenets of Dataism is that we should willingly give all of the data pertaining to ourselves to Google and other tech companies because they will then know more about ourselves than we possibly can. They will therefore make "better" decisions for us! What "better" means is of course open to strenuous debate. Religion indeed! The trust one is required to place in technology and tech companies strains one's credibility! Shades of Splitting and Melanie Klein!

With the preceding in mind, I turn to the ethics of large-scale, complex, messy systems. Unfortunately, in the vast majority of cases, any serious consideration of ethics is seriously lacking.

Notes

1. Alex Peysakhovich and Seth Stephens-Davidowitz, "How Not to Drown in Numbers," *The New York Times*, Sunday, May 3, 2015, pp. 6–7.
2. Homo Deus, op. cit.

8

The Ethics of Complex Messy Systems

Wicked messes raise profound issues of ethics and morality. Wicked messes are not just composed of complex technical issues and problems, but they are deep entanglements of complex ethical issues as well, namely, what are the "'right' things that we ought to do with regard to all of the serious issues facing us?"

Three Major Schools/Traditions

Three major schools/traditions are predominant in ethics: virtues, utilitarianism, and deontology. The virtue school stresses that to be ethical means possessing the right set of attributes, for example, honesty, trustworthiness, and strength of character. In terms of technology, this means that technology and technologists are inherently virtuous, an attitude that we shall see that is one of the cornerstones of The Technological Mindset.

Portion of Chapters Four through Nine appeared previously as blogs in The Huffington Post.

I. I. Mitroff, *Technology Run Amok*,
https://doi.org/10.1007/978-3-319-95741-8_8

In the twentieth century, Utilitarianism has taken the form of cost-benefit analysis. In this system, something is ethical if the benefits associated with the acts it sanctions exceed the costs or disbenefits. As we shall also see, this way of thinking assumes a perverse form in The Technological Mindset where only the positive benefits associated with technology are typically considered. Indeed, according to The Technological Mindset, technology is positive through and through. The disbenefits are minor, if they exist at all.

The school/tradition associated with deontology stresses the inherent goodness or rightness of a set of actions, considerations, or principles themselves. For instance, the contention is often wrongly made that technology is ethically neutral. That is, technology can be used for good or evil ends or purposes, and which it's used for is not the inherent responsibility of technologists. This all-too conveniently ignores the fact that all technologies are created with certain desired ends in mind, ends that are anything but neutral. The contention that technology is neutral is more an expression of the fact that technologists are reluctant to engage in any serious exploration of the consequences of their prized creations.

While important to be sure, this brief discussion of the main schools/traditions of ethics glosses over one of the most vital aspects of ethics, ethical reasoning. The reasoning that one uses to reach, and even more to justify, a set of actions or principles as being ethical is extremely, if not all, important. Let me therefore turn to a particular example which while on the surface is far removed from technology turns out to have a great bearing on it. In fact, it's a powerful expression of a commonly held principle, namely passing the ethical buck. In short, "if someone else takes up the slack in worrying about whether something is ethical or not, then I don't have to worry about it." As we shall see, this is one of the cornerstones of The Technological Mindset as well.

The point is that the field of ethics is anything but a bounded, linear, straightforward, and well-structured exercise. More often than not, we elicit ethical principles by examining cases that are far removed from the primary situation with which we are interested. Once elicited, we then explore whether the same principle applies to that which is our primary concern.

Ethical Reasoning: An Example

The April 13, 2015, issue of *TIME* contains one of the most powerful examples of ethical reasoning. It featured a strong interchange between two arguments, pro and con (pp. 32–33), over whether Indiana's Religious Freedom Restoration Act is necessary or not. The issues at the heart of the debate are: Are the beliefs of orthodox Christians so much under attack such that they deserve special protection? Should orthodox Christians and the members of other faiths be required to undertake actions with which go against their fundamental beliefs? Specifically, should the owners of businesses be forced to serve those—for example, gays who wish to be married or who already are—that violate their deeply held religious beliefs?

The parallels with technology are not hard to draw. Does technology deserve special protection because to technologists it is always on the verge of being under attack, if it's not already?

I found the proposition by Rod Dreher, a Senior Editor of *The American Conservative*, not only seriously flawed, but utterly contemptible. In the interests of clarification, I've recast just one of the critical parts of Dreher's argument into the form of various ethical propositions. This is one of the most powerful ways of which I know for analyzing any argument. In other words, each of the various components of the Toulmin Argumentation Framework—Claims, Evidence, Warrants, Backings, and Rebuttals—is deeply infused with ethical propositions and commitments of some sort.

According to my reading of Pragmatism, the particular philosophical school in which I was schooled and favor, "Truth is that which makes an Ethical difference in the Quality of one's life." Thus, according to Pragmatism, truth (epistemology, the methods and processes used by humans arrive at knowledge and truth), ethics (what are the "right things we ought to do"), and aesthetics (what is pleasing, harmonious, etc.) are inseparable, where the term "quality" is a proxy for aesthetics. Further, the little word "makes" means that according to Pragmatism, we do not have truth until we actually implement an ethical action that is carefully designed to deal with, and hopefully lessen, an important problem. Pragmatism is thus fundamentally systemic.

In the spirit of Immanuel Kant (who is often associated with, if not credited with establishing, the school of deontology), putting arguments in the form of ethical propositions forces us to ask, "Can this particular ethical maxim be generalized such that we'd want it to be applied universally to all persons?" Or, "Is it so odious that common human decency forces us to reject it as strongly as possible?"

It's not the case that my ethical and moral standards are above reproach or universal. Far from it. The point is that an ethical proposition of some sort underlies every important social and technical issue. As such, they need to be fleshed out so that they can be subject to rigorous examination. Ideally, this is a case where More Leads to More.

Let me take one of Dreher's prime contentions, namely, that if one baker refuses for whatever personal or religious reasons to make a wedding cake for a gay couple, in today's world there are many more bakers who are willing to have their business; therefore, gay couples have no right to feel slighted and thus complain. Translated into an ethical proposition, the principle reads:

> "Whenever there is at least one other person, say person 2, who is willing to serve person 1, who for whatever reasons person 3 refuses to serve, then person 3 is justified ethically in refusing service to person 1. In other words, person 3 is justified ethically in committing an act of discrimination." To boil it down, "discrimination in the large is acceptable as long as there is at least one person in the small as it were who doesn't practice it."

This dubious principle not only further institutionalizes prejudice, but it also puts the burden squarely on those who have been discriminated against to seek out others who do not engage in discrimination. Worst of all, the principle serves as its own justification. It conveniently sidesteps the whole issue where there is no one in a small or closed community who wishes to serve someone else. Should the person who is denied service then be forced to drive miles at considerable cost and time in order to find someone who will serve them?

In Dreher's words, "What is so alarming about the opposition's [presumably, Liberals and gays] moral panic over [the Indiana law] is its inability to accept that there could possibly be a legitimate religious defense of discrimination at all." Really? Name one! Slavery and the treatment of blacks and women? To discriminate among ideas is one thing—people, quite another. It's one of the worst forms of Splitting imaginable. This does not mean that there are never any good or valid reasons for condemning the actions and beliefs of a particular group such as ISIS.

I accept of course that anyone is free to believe anything they wish, but not necessarily to say publically, especially not hate speech. (To put it mildly, defining what is and what is not "hate speech" is difficult. This precisely why I discuss the topic of Inquiry Systems later. Namely, which systems of Inquiry are best suited to tackling messy, difficult to define issues?) But, since businesses are licensed by law to serve the general public, one's actions are subject to a different standard. In this case, the proposition that "Every belief and action that is based on one's deeply held personal or religious beliefs are warranted ethically" fails in my judgment miserably.

In the end, the Indiana law is just the latest skirmish in the long and seemingly never-ending battle against the dark and repressive forces that we have fought throughout all of human history. The dubious principles on which discrimination are based do not hold up to the moral cleansing light of daylight.

The Odious Concept of Ethical Thresholds

Consider a more recent case. Putting one of the prime justifications for President Trump's policy toward banning Muslims in the form of a generalized ethical proposition shows how odiously undeveloped his sense of ethics is: "Whenever the numbers of people who are detained from entering a country are small in comparison to those who are let in, then one is warranted ethically in enacting such a policy." In other words, "Whenever the numbers of people who are harmed by a policy are small, the policy is warranted." To which a good Kantian would reply, "To harm even one person is to harm all the members of society for the principle cannot be generalized such that it leads to a just world."

Worst of all, the proposition dignifies the dangerous concept an ethical threshold. As long as the numbers of people who are hurt are below some magic number, then our actions are ethical. This only raises the treacherous question, "How many would have to be hurt before one's actions are deemed unethical?" All of this is not only morally odious to a Kantian, but extremely dangerous.

Yes, weighing the benefits versus the disbenefits of any proposed action is the hallmark of Utilitarian Ethics, and as such, always tugs at us. For who can be oblivious to benefits versus costs, especially if the costs are cataclysmic? But while it must always be taken seriously, Utilitarianism can never be the sole basis for acting ethically for it invariably leads to the odious concept of ethical thresholds. Therefore, there must be other bases. And, since Utilitarianism is the underlying ethical basis of The Technological Mindset, it's vitally important that we note its shortcomings.

In those societies that strive to be just, they struggle to arrive at and practice a set of principles each of which is just in and of itself. Thus, a person applying for entry is to be judged primarily on his or her individual merits, not on their country of origin, race, religion, etc. Whether a person can support one's self or requires help, affirms primary allegiance to the country to which he or she is applying, and especially to its democratic principles, etc., are potentially legitimate criteria, depending of course on how they are actually implemented. In other words, the criteria for admittance must not be rigged against particular countries or groups unless it can be demonstrated beyond all reasonable doubt that the members of a particular group such as ISIS are irredeemably dangerous. The burden of proof is thus intentionally set high for he or she who would impose barriers.

Passing the Ethical Buck and Technology

Unfortunately, the principle of passing the ethical buck applies with equal force to technology. In effect, the underlying argument is:

> Whenever third parties (say parents, teachers, etc.) are available to monitor the behavior of young users (second parties), then the developers of

a technology (first parties) are off the hook ethically with regard to the potentially harmful effects of a technology.

Thus, the burden is placed squarely on unorganized groups of parents, teachers, etc., who can't be available 24/7/365 to monitor the behavior of young children when it comes to their uses of technology and thereby counter the power of organized interests who are not always interested in the well-being of kids. For example, parents should carefully monitor the "screen times" of their children. To say that this principle is dubious doesn't even begin to say how odious it is.

Making Connections: The Moral Imperative of Our Times

Thinking and acting systemically are key. It is in fact the supreme moral imperative of our times. It means acknowledging that the major schools of ethics in Western societies were formulated when ethics was principally a matter of the rightful conduct between a small number of individual actors or agents with clearly foreseeable benefits versus disbenefits.

In contrast, thinking and acting systemically means asking among many things, "As best as one can determine, who are all the parties who will benefit as well as be hurt the most by any proposed action?" This in turn requires the ability to see and to acknowledge the intended and unintended consequences of one's actions. In short, it requires the ability to make connections.

In a world that is interconnected along every conceivable dimension, the ability to foresee and to make important connections is more vital than ever. Indeed, only those who have the ability to make important connections will survive, let alone prosper.

For instance, because we'd all be forced to pay higher prices for food, proposed tariffs on Mexican goods are a direct tax on American consumers. The country imposing tariffs thus has as much, if not more, to lose than the country being targeted.

Slowing down and preventing Muslims from entering the country hurts the USA in that it alienates Muslims worldwide. Just when their cooperation is needed more than ever, there is less incentive to help a government that is viewed as inherently hostile. It only furthers the fear that banning Muslims plays directly into the hands of ISIS, which it has. It also encourages long-time allies to rethink their commitments to the USA.

As odious as Republicans find the Affordable Care Act, getting rid of it poses severe problems. For one, it threatens to blow up insurance markets, for what will be the size of the remaining pool of people able to afford coverage, and who will they be, both of which are crucial in determining premiums? For another, millions who have had coverage, often for the first time, are threatened with losing it. Even though the recent Republican healthcare bill was defeated by the enormous push-back by those who would be actually hurt by it, the potential political damage to Republicans is far from over.

Despite the fact that over 97% of reputable climate scientists world-wide believe on the basis of sound science that humans are primarily responsible for global warming, far too many still vehemently deny the connection, and thereby the entire phenomenon. Unfortunately, by the time they finally admit it, it'll be too late to do anything serious about it.

With the exception of global warming, none of the preceding propositions are automatically or conclusively true. Every one of them is highly contentious, a fact that is generally true of all important issues. Indeed, the matter is easily turned on its head: Something is important if and only if it provokes intense differences of opinion.

The Age of Uncertain, World-Changing Connections

Obviously, one's level of education, political affiliation, ideology, raw intelligence, etc., all play critical roles in determining whether one sees potential interactions. Although it's tempting to portray conservatives and Republicans as least likely to acknowledge interactions, especially the more complex they are, liberals with narrow worldviews are unable to admit them as well. For this reason, it's patently false to single out any particular group.

The ability to think expansively is more critical than ever. We are firmly in The Age of Uncertain, World-Changing Connections.

This does not mean that we should take seriously, let alone accept, every proposed connection, least of all those that are the result of conspiracy theorists, the purveyors of Fake News, or "alternative facts." It means that traditional forms of handling and portraying complex issues are no longer adequate. We need outlets that can display side by side the opposing arguments and evidence for and against important connections. It's no longer sufficient to turn to separate sources to get the arguments pro and con for important issues. This does not mean opposing "talking heads" as is the norm now. It means laying out systematically the evidence pro and con for important issues.

Dialectic Reasoning

It's not that both sides of important issues necessarily need to be equally credible, but that one of the most important ways of determining what's credible is by viewing the strongest case that can be made for and against any important proposition. The issues we face are too important not to be examined in such a manner. In a word, dialectic reasoning needs to be front and center. It's the foundation for ethical thinking in a complex, dangerous world. I say more about this in a later chapter.

Concluding Remarks

The next chapter shows that all of the issues involved with innovation and technology raise profound ethical issues. The results of this chapter thus apply with equal force.

9

How Technology Both Enhances and Diminishes Our Humanity

Let me begin with two quotes that speak directly to the major themes of this chapter:

> If we continue to develop our technology without wisdom or prudence, our servant may prove to be our Executioner.[1] (Omar N. Bradly)

> The people who work on News Feed aren't making decisions that turn on fuzzy human ideas like ethics, judgment, intuition, or seniority. They are concerned only with quantifiable outcomes about people's actions on the site. That data, at Facebook, is the only real truth. And it is a particular kind of truth: The News Feed team's ultimate mission is to figure out what users want—what they find 'meaningful' to use Cox and Zuckerberg's preferred term—and to give them more of that.[2] (Farhad Manjoo)

There is no other way to approach the matter but to say it outright: Technology Is Run Amok! In short, it's out of control.

Portion of Chapters Four through Nine appeared previously as blogs in The Huffington Post.

© The Author(s) 2019
I. I. Mitroff, *Technology Run Amok*,
https://doi.org/10.1007/978-3-319-95741-8_9

Technology not only greatly enhances, but it also greatly diminishes our humanity. As a result, it is one of the biggest threats facing humankind.[3] It may well be the biggest threat or potential crisis of all. As Stephanie Brown has put it, not only are we highly dependent on technology, but worse, we've become deeply addicted to it.[4] Technology is one of the most pernicious forms of More Leads to Less.

When technology serves legitimate human needs and desires, then of course it's a tremendous boon to humanity, but when it exacerbates and creates false needs, it's a curse. Continually clarifying the differences between "legitimate" and "false" needs is one of the most important, ongoing tasks facing us. This is one of the prime reasons for using the right Inquiry System to make such judgments.

More specifically, what I call The Technological Mindset, which I describe shortly, constitutes a major threat to humanity. In brief, The Technological Mindset is a set of mutually reinforcing beliefs that not only assert the primacy, but the superiority of technology in dealing with and mastering every aspect of human affairs. For instance, technology is the solution to every problem. Never mind that technology creates many problems to which it's supposedly its own solution. For another, innovation and technology are supreme positive goods that must be protected at all costs. (Shades of the last chapter.) Hence, they must be subject to as few constraints and regulations as possible.

In asserting that innovation and technology are nothing but supreme positive goods, The Technological Mindset is merely stating what to it is an obvious, if not a given, truth. What it fails to realize is that all of its so-called truths are barely disguised ethical allegations. At the very least, they are shot through and through with ethical commitments of various kinds. They do more than merely state how the world "is." More basic, they proclaim how it "ought to be." Instead of each of its so-called truths being factual or logically true propositions, they are instead highly debatable, if not dubious, ethical contentions. Indeed, it's using variants of all three of the major schools/traditions of ethics at the same time.

Identifying the full set of assertions/beliefs that make up The Technological Mindset is not only a crucial task, but it's in fact the first step in our regaining control of technology for the betterment of humankind. However, for this very reason, I find it most disturbing that the key elements of The Technological Mindset are scattered at best.[5]

Despite the many who are highly critical of technology, as well as those who are strongly supportive of it, The Technological Mindset has not been organized, and therefore not examined, as a set of mutually reinforcing beliefs, i.e., as an interrelated belief system. But then the dis-aggregation of thoughts and ideas is one of the prime features of The Technological Mindset. Even though it's a set of mutually reinforcing beliefs, The Technological Mindset treats everything, including itself, as if were nothing more than a set of independent, self-standing beliefs. Further, this mind-set is so deeply ingrained in Western culture such that even those who are highly critical of it are under its spell no less. Notwithstanding all my criticisms, I am no less subject to it as well.

The Better Management of Technology

As I've emphasized throughout, I am not suggesting in the slightest that we would somehow all be better off without all of the marvelous tech-nologies that make our lives incomparably better. Instead, I am calling for the improved ethical management of technology. As I've stressed throughout, before we unleash the latest great technologies in the world, we need to assess as carefully as we can its social impacts, both negative and positive, and to do everything we can to guard against, and thus mitigate, the negative impacts before it's too late to do anything responsible about them. But to do this, one must not only confront The Technological Mindset as a total interrelated system of beliefs, but offer reasonable alternatives to it. I offer one in the next chapter.

Unfortunately, as we shall see shortly, merely contemplating, let alone assessing systematically, the potential negative impacts of technology, is not one of the key elements of The Technological Mindset. Indeed, The Technological Mindset not only focuses solely on the positive, but it absolutely rhapsodizes them. As a result, it not only precludes, but resists serious discussions of the negative.

The Technological Mindset

The key elements of The Technological Mindset are given below. I have assembled them from a wide variety of sources.[6] Roughly half are highly critical of technology while the others are extremely positive. Since they differ in their interpretations of key elements, in assembling such a list, it's not only important to draw upon those who are highly critical of a belief system, but those who are highly supportive of it as well. They also identify somewhat different elements as well.

While the order of the items is not absolutely crucial per se, I have organized them such that they generally build upon one another. In a sense, they constitute a natural progression. More importantly, the wordings of the items are not neutral for neither the critics nor the supporters of The Technological Mindset are neutral with regard to each and every one of its components. In this regard, I have tried as best I can to capture the underlying "spirit" of each of the elements.

Furthermore, make no mistake about it. The following are extreme statements of an extreme worldview. This is not to say that all scientists and technologists necessarily endorse all of the items, certainly not in their extreme form. Nonetheless, given my reading of the literature, many do. Whatever the case, all of the propositions are highly contentious.

Furthermore, as extreme as The Technological Mindset is, it pales in comparison with Yuval Noah Harari's *Homo Deus*.[7] It's one of the most extreme statements concerning the role and superiority of technology that I've ever encountered.

Finally, precisely because The Technological Mindset is so extreme, many will undoubtedly dismiss it as a straw man. This is exactly what one should not do. Its implications are important such that it needs to be taken with the upmost seriousness:

1. Technology is the single most important factor responsible for material and economic progress. Without constant technological innovation, there can be no material and economic prosperity, period!

2. Not only does every problem have a solution, but technology is the solution to all problems. In fact, the answer to the problems caused by any technology is always more technology.
3. Constant innovation and technology are essential activities and supreme goods that must be protected at all costs. There must be as few constraints and limits placed on innovation and technology as possible. Government regulations must be fought tooth and nail! For instance, the Internet must be totally free and unencumbered.
4. Technological progress is inevitable. Not only is it futile to resist innovation and technology, but it's extremely dangerous and wrong-headed to do so.
5. The positive attributes and/or effects of any proposed innovation or technology are paramount. In other words, only the positive effects are important in contemplating any proposed innovation or technology. As such, technologists must not be "bogged down" by unnecessary ruminations about negative consequences. The social consequences of technology are not only secondary, but should not be the primary concern of technologists. They have more important things to consider.
6. One should not be unduly concerned about those whose jobs are displaced or rendered obsolete by technology for there will always be new jobs and industries, if only for those who are willing to learn new high-level skills.
7. Utilitarianism is the prevailing ethic that should form the basis for all decisions regarding the fate of new technologies. Issues of efficiency, not justice and human dignity, are paramount. If the benefits exceed the costs or disbenefits, then a technology is ethically warranted.
8. Concrete metrics and scales are to be constructed and used in making all key decisions. In other words, quantification is not only to be used in all cases, but is unequivocally superior to qualitative judgments. Thus, in principle, all complex decisions are capable of being reduced to algorithms, that is, integrated assemblages of quantitative rules. Algorithms are preferable for they make key decisions objectively and impartially.

9. Capitalism is <u>the</u> superior economic system bar none. In some limited cases, funds may have to be set aside for displaced workers.
10. The increased use of robots is not only inevitable, but eminently desirable. Robots are in principle capable of taking over and doing all jobs better, i.e., smarter, and more efficiently. Robots are not only more efficient but more dependable and reliable. For instance, they are better suited in caring for the elderly and sick than humans who don't want to be bothered by them.
11. It's not only inevitable but highly desirable that machines will soon exceed human intelligence.
12. It's only a deep-seated, long-standing, irrational human prejudice that refuses to grant machines the same attributes and qualities that have been reserved for humans. There are no valid reasons why machines cannot think, feel, and display human-like emotions. Indeed, a new vocabulary has to be created to put machine-like attributes on an equal par with humans. In order to advance their acceptance, robots should look as human as possible.
13. The fact that we are already cyborgs—and becoming more so with every passing day—is to be celebrated. The depth and level to which technology will and should be parts of the human race are without limit. At best, humans need to be augmented by having chips and devices implanted in them. In the end, humans will be obsolete and be replaced by robots.
14. The ultimate hope is that we live long enough until biomedical technology has advanced to the point such that we will be the last generation to die!
15. Not only will humans adapt as they always have, but it's their duty to adapt to technology! Indeed, they have no choice but to adapt!

Technology Has Become the New God

All of the above are not only highly contestable and problematic, but in many cases, they are directly at odds with one another, if not out-and-out contradictory. For instance, of necessity, all of the elements of The

Technological Mindset are highly qualitative, ethical judgments. Thus, for all its worship of quantitative thinking, The Technological Mindset depends, as all belief systems do, on highly qualitative judgments that are taken to be "true" without exception or limitation. They rest on the highly questionable dictum that "If all of human progress rests fundamentally on technology, then protecting it at all costs is the supreme ethic to which all human actions and decisions must be subject." Every part of this Claim is debatable. Human progress depends as much, if not more, on the existence and well-being of democratic institutions as it does on technology.

To its believers, each and every one of the elements of The Technological Mindset is an absolute moral truth. Technology embodies all of the virtues of supreme goodness and righteousness. Unlike those who live in a universe where truth and ethics are separate and distinct, humans generally live in a world where their truths are "true" because they are "moral." They not only state what the world is like, but even more, what it ought to be. Indeed, what it has to be like.

In a word, technology has become a new God, a God that all of us should worship without any reservations whatsoever. All of the highest attributes and qualities—virtues—that were once reserved for God have now become fundamental properties of technology. Technology has taken on an aura of supreme goodness, ultra perfection, super intelligence, immortality, etc.

Managing the Social Impacts of Technology

As I've argued, a technology should be adopted if and only if it continues to pass the most severe social impact audits we can muster. The burden is thus placed squarely on technologists to justify their inventions and to ensure that the negative impacts are under control.

Further, if only for the reason that technologists are generally resistant to the idea of social audits, we cannot leave them to voluntary compliance. They have to be made mandatory. This is another part of the prime ethical constraints to which all technologies need to be subject. Indeed, I believe that a new government agency equivalent to the FDA needs to be created to continually monitor all technologies for their potential ill effects. Further, since so many technologies impact children and young adults, I also believe that as a prime stakeholder group, parents need to take the lead in forming a new organization to pressure the government to oversee technology.

Artificial Intelligence (AI)

One of the most highly contentious issues in The Technological Mindset is not only whether computers can "think," but whether they can replicate, let alone exceed, the critical traits associated with human intelligence, especially those that are reserved for higher-order skills such as creative thought. To date, computers regularly beat grand masters at chess. They can even "write" short articles on various subjects once they have been fed certain sets of background data and facts. Whether such articles are "creative" is of course what separates the supporters of AI from its detractors. And, computers have even bested previous winners of the popular game show Jeopardy.

Computers are able to do these things because the "rules" that humans follow to achieve high performance have not only been studied extensively, but distilled into programs that computers then use to "simulate" human thought. The critical question is of course whether human thought, let alone intelligence, is nothing but a set of rules, however refined and sophisticated they may be. In other words, can human thought be reduced to a set of rules? Because if it can, and if the rules can be encoded into computers, then computers can be said to "think."

All of this is just fodder for the debate. If once again the body is not merely "a sophisticated carrying case for the brain," and therefore that thought is a property of the entire mind/body system, then human thought does not take place entirely in the brain alone. Further, if thoughts and emotions are not separable—there are no thoughts without emotions and vice versa—then human thought is not just a matter of capturing rules (contrary to Sensing Thinking or ST, Intuitive Thinking or NT), but it also consists of feelings that are the antithesis of rules (Intuitive Feeling or NF, Sensing Feeling or SF). In this sense, computers cannot, and perhaps never will, "think." Sara Manning Peskin has put the matter well: "The human body's most compassionate gift is the interdependence of its parts."[8]

All of this is further complicated by the fact that much of human thought—the mind itself—is unconscious (hence, the importance of Freud and Melanie Klein). This makes the "rules" much harder to capture for many of them are not available to conscious thought.

This is not to say that much has not been learned about thought by studying rules and programming computers to simulate human thought. But then, that's also what the debate is all about.

In the end, the debate is more about ethics than it is about technology. Do we really want computers to take over activities that have been the exclusive province of humans? And of course, there are the real fears that computers will take over and subdue humans in ways of which we're completely unaware, and thus before it's too late to do anything about it.

Can Humans Be Replaced by Robots? Should They?

The same debate is played out concerning the role of robots. Since in growing numbers of cases, robots are more efficient, reliable, and dependable than humans, should we therefore turn more and more of human work over to robots? And, where at all possible, should humans be eliminated altogether?

All of this is complicated by the fact that more and more activities once thought to be capable of only being done humans are now capable of being performed by "intelligent robots." For instance, robots are no longer restricted to moving large, bulky containers around huge factory floors. Not only can they pick up and sort thin pieces of paper that require enormous dexterity and touch, but they can perform higher-order tasks that require decision-making. Thus, it's not inconceivable that robots will replace bank tellers, financial planners, and even medical doctors. Of course, since making and sustaining emotional connections (SF) are a big part of medical care, it's highly contestable whether medical doctors can ever be fully replaced by robots.

If robots can replace humans, then the potential economic advantages to businesses are enormous (ST). But once again, should this be the sole criterion for replacing humans? The consideration of robots not only raises profound ethical questions, but the fundamental question of what kind of a society in which we wish to live (NF).

Should those businesses that opt for robots be required to pay for programs to train and retrain displaced workers for new jobs? I argue that they should. This is another of the strong ethical propositions concerning the limits of technology to which I subscribe.

Further, I would limit the use of robots to tasks that are too dangerous for humans to perform and that which they choose not to do.

Notes

1. Goodman, op. cit., p. 25.
2. Farhad Manjoo, "Social Insecurity," *The New York Times Magazine*, April 30, 2017, p. 43.
3. Jasanoff, op. cit.
4. Brown, op. cit.
5. TTM is scattered among the following: Erik Brynjolfsson and Anrew McAfee, *The Second Machine Age: Work, Progress, and Personality in a Time of Brilliant Technologies*, Norton, New York, 2014; Andy Clark, *Natural-Born Cyborgs: Minds, Technologies, and the Future of Human Intelligence*, Oxford University Press, New York, 2003; Martin Ford, *Rise of the Robots: Technology and the Threat of a Jobless Future*, Basic Books, New York, 2015; Thomas Frank, *Listen Liberal: Or, What Ever Happened to the Party of the People?*, Metropolitan Books, New York, 2016; Andrew Keen, *The Internet Is Not the Answer*, Atlantic Monthly Press, New York, 2015; Evegny Morozov, *To Save Everything, Click Here: The Folly of Technological Solutionism*, Public Affairs, New York, 2013; Alec Ross, *The Industries of the Future*, Simon and Schuster, New York, 2016; and Sherry Turkle, *Alone Together: Why We Expect More from Technology and Less from Each Other*, Basic Books, New York, 2011.
6. Ibid.

7. *Homo Deus*, op. cit.
8. Sara Manning Peskin, "The Gentler Symptoms of Dying," *The New York Times*, July 18, 2017, p. D6.

10

Contesting The Technological Mindset: A Humanistic Mindset

I want to contest every element of The Technological Mindset with strong Rebuttals in the form of Counter Claims. Taken together, the Counter Claims constitute A Humanistic Mindset. They also constitute one side of one of the most important dialectics with which we must continually cope:

1. *Claim*: Technology is the single most important factor responsible for material and economic progress. Without constant technological innovation, there can be no material and economic prosperity, period!

   Counter Claim: No one seriously disputes the fact that technology is an extremely important factor in human affairs. But, without appropriate social institutions both to nurture and to support it, technology cannot even exist, let alone contribute to material and economic progress. Contributing to the total well-being of society is even more of a challenge. Notice carefully that in terms of the Myers-Briggs, the Counter Claim is a forceful expression of Intuitive Feeling (NF) and Sensing Feeling (SF). As we shall see, this is generally true of all of the Counter Claims.

© The Author(s) 2019
I. I. Mitroff, *Technology Run Amok*,
https://doi.org/10.1007/978-3-319-95741-8_10

If technology is the "brain" of society, then social institutions are its "body and mind." This is also NF.

The great danger is mistaking one variable, and one variable alone, for the whole of a mess, let alone for its most important component. This is clearly Intuitive Thinking (NT).

2. *Claim*: Not only does every problem have a solution, but technology is the solution to all problems. In fact, the answer to the problems caused by any technology is always more technology.

   Counter Claim: Problems are parts of messes. As such, they do not have "solutions" per se. We only "cope" with messes, never fully "solve them." The situation is even worse for Wicked Messes.

   Technology is just one component of every mess (NT). This is not to dispute that it's a very important component, but it's not always the most important one. Instead, our attitudes toward technology and the kinds of societies in which we wish to live are every bit as important, if not more so (NF).

3. *Claim*: Constant innovation and technology are essential activities and supreme goods that must be protected at all costs. There must be as few constraints and limits placed on innovation and technology as possible. Government regulations must be fought tooth and nail! For instance, the Internet must be totally free and unencumbered.

   Counter Claim: There is no such thing as "society" without constraints and limits. Setting appropriate constraints and limits is one of the basic functions, if not key defining attributes, of "society."

4. *Claim*: Technological progress is inevitable. Not only is it futile to resist innovation and technology, but it's extremely dangerous and wrongheaded to do so.

   Counter Claim: All technologies are not uniformly good, certainly not in all of their aspects. All technologies must be subject to ongoing social impact audits as well as government regulations. Those that are injurious or result in large-scale disruption must be carefully monitored and controlled.

5. *Claim*: The positive attributes and/or effects of any proposed innovation or technology are paramount. In other words, only the positive effects are important in contemplating any proposed innovation

or technology. As such, technologists must not be "bogged down" by unnecessary ruminations about negative consequences. The social consequences of technology are not only secondary, but are not and should not be the primary concern of technologists. They have more important things to consider.

Counter Claim: The social consequences of technology are primary. What's the point of any technology if it causes harm?

There is nothing that doesn't have negative as well as positive consequences. By definition, all wicked messes have both negative and positive attributes.

Before any technology is unleashed on the world, it must be subject to an intense crisis audit (see the next chapter) that deliberately probes for potential ill effects. Mitigation plans must be carefully undertaken to counteract potential ill effects.

6. *Claim*: One should not be unduly concerned about those whose jobs are displaced or rendered obsolete by technology for there will always be new jobs and industries for those, if only for those, who are willing to learn new high-level skills.

   Counter Claim: One should be especially concerned about those who are displaced by any technology (NF, SF). Funds need to be created for those who are displaced (ST, NT). The innovators of any new technology need to pay into such funds. They need to be a basic part of the development and continuing costs of any technology.

   In those cases where sizable numbers of workers are certain to be displaced, and cannot be easily retrained, then it's not clear whether a technology should be adopted merely because it's more efficient or economic. Giving people meaningful employment (NF, SF) is more important than economic savings (NT, ST). This is another of the prime ethical principles to which I subscribe.

7. *Claim*: Utilitarianism is the prevailing ethic that should form the basis for all decisions regarding the fate of new technologies. Issues of efficiency, not justice and human dignity, are paramount. If the benefits exceed the costs or disbenefits, then a technology is ethically warranted.

   Counter Claim: Utilitarianism is not the only ethic that humans have devised. Enhancing and preserving human dignity are paramount. Ethical systems differ precisely on the role they accord to human dignity.

8. *Claim*: Concrete metrics and scales are to be constructed and used in making all key decisions. In other words, quantification is not only to be used in all cases, but is unequivocally superior to qualitative judgments. Thus, in principle, all complex decisions are capable of being reduced to algorithms, that is, integrated assemblages of quantitative rules. Algorithms are preferable for they make key decisions objectively and impartially.

   Counter Claim: The Claim is self-contradictory for it's a qualitative statement about the supposed superiority of quantitative reasoning. Qualitative judgments precede all quantitative assessments.

   Algorithms are not necessarily, let alone inherently, "objective," for they embody the biases and value judgments of their creators.[1] In many cases, they promote and further economic and social inequality.

9. *Claim*: Capitalism is <u>the</u> superior economic system, bar none. In some limited cases, funds may have to be set aside for displaced workers.

   Counter Claim: Pure Capitalism never has and never will exist. There are no market economies without strong governments to set the rules of the game.

   The real reason why Capitalism is favored is the dream that one's inventions will rack up billions of dollars.

10. *Claim*: The increased use of robots is not only inevitable, but eminently desirable. Robots are in principle capable of taking over and doing all jobs better, i.e., smarter, and more efficiently. Robots are not only more efficient but more dependable and reliable. For instance, they are better suited in caring for the elderly and sick than humans who don't want to be bothered by them.

    Counter Claim: Not all of human thought can be reduced to rules and algorithms (NF, SF). Robots cannot do everything that we take to be human.

11. *Claim*: It's not only inevitable but highly desirable that machines will soon exceed human intelligence.

Counter Claim: The counter to this Claim is provided in the previous chapter. In short, not all of human intelligence can be captured in rules. Emotional intelligence (SF, NF) is just as important cognitive intelligence (ST, NT).

12. *Claim*: It's only a deep-seated, long-standing, irrational human prejudice that refuses to grant machines the same attributes and qualities that have been reserved for humans. There are no valid reasons why machines cannot think, feel, and display human-like emotions. Indeed, a new vocabulary has to be created to put machine-like qualities on an equal par with humans. In order to advance their acceptance, robots should look as human as possible.
    Counter Claim: The previous chapter provides a counter to this Claim as well. In short, SF and NF cannot be reduced to ST and NT.

13. *Claim*: The fact that we are already cyborgs—and becoming more so with every passing day—is to be celebrated. The depth and level to which technology will and should be parts of the human race are without limit. At best, humans need to be augmented by having chips and devices implanted in them. In the end, humans will be obsolete and be replaced by robots.
    Counter Claim: The previous chapter provides a counter to this Claim. It represents nothing less than the complete devaluation of humans.

14. *Claim*: The ultimate hope is that we live long enough until biomedical technology has advanced to the point such that we will be the last generation to die!
    Counter Claim: Death is an important part of life (no pun intended), and of being human as we have known it. Talk about the need for social impact analyses if we ever are the last generation to die! The social consequences—read "crises"—are enormous.

15. *Claim*: Not only will humans adapt as they always have, but it's their duty to adapt to technology! Indeed, they have no choice but to adapt!
    Counter Claim: Why must it be that humans should always be the ones to adapt to technologies and not the other way around?

Note

1. Cathy O'Neil, *Weapons of Math Destruction: How Big Data Increases Inequality and Threatens Democracy,* Crown, New York, 2016.

11

Crisis Management: Coping with Technology

The modern field of crisis management (CM) began in 1982 with the deaths of seven people in a suburb outside of Chicago due to the cyanide poisoning of Tylenol capsules. It was the preeminent case of product tampering.

Because I had worked as a consultant to McNeil Pharmaceuticals, the makers of Tylenol, and further since I'd found it to be an ethical company, I was immediately drawn to CM. I am in fact one of the field's principal founders.

The Different Types of Crises

Although I did not fully realize it at the time, there were a number of important steps in the creation of a new field. The most immediate was not just the definition of a crisis (ST), but an understanding of the various kinds and types of crises (NT, NF). While product tampering was certainly the most important, it was, and still is, only one of the many different kinds of crises. The recognition of others followed quickly. Thus, there are informational crises where someone deliberately tampers

© The Author(s) 2019
I. I. Mitroff, *Technology Run Amok*,
https://doi.org/10.1007/978-3-319-95741-8_11

with private records, or sells them to third parties for profit, that could harm individuals, business, and governments, for instance, cyber hacking and the 2016 presidential election. Facebook's well-documented crisis due to its shady dealings with Cambridge Analytica is a primary example as well.

There are technological crises as in the case where a chemical power plant explodes, causes deaths, and widespread destruction. The more general case is where a technology causes irreversible harm to animals, the environment, humans, plants, etc. And, of course it also includes all of the various kinds of crises due to technology that we have been discussing.

There are ethical crises as in the case of Volkswagen where an organization deliberatively deceives its customers about the true levels of toxic pollutants that are emitted from its vehicles. This in turn led inevitably to public relations (PR) crises. Wells Fargo committed the same in opening unauthorized accounts for millions of people. Once again, it includes Facebook's dubious ethics with regard to its allowing Cambridge Analytica to have unauthorized access to the personal information of millions of its users.

All in all, my colleagues and I identified some 12–14 different types or general "families of crises."

The next realization occurred when it became clear that it was never enough to prepare for one and only one type of crisis. All of the different types were intimately related. Any one type of crisis was capable of setting off a chain reaction that resulted in all of the others. Volkswagen is just a recent example. What started as a PR Crisis soon led to a financial crisis (it's reported that it will cost VW some 11 billion dollars and counting!), a leadership/ethical crisis, and so on. In other words, when it comes to CM, the necessity for engaging in Systems Thinking is not just crucial, but it's an absolute necessity. Since Systems Thinking is one of the preeminent types of Inquiry Systems, understanding them is also an absolute requirement. For this reason, I describe the special role of Inquiry Systems in a later chapter.

To take another example, one doesn't have to tell the chemical industry to prepare for fires and explosions for that's a normal part of its everyday business. The problem is that as a technology-based industry, it has trouble learning that it needs to prepare for crises that are primarily human-caused such as PR and ethical crises. It has even more difficulty accepting that all crises are human-caused, especially so-called natural disasters. After all, it is humans, not Mother Nature, who make the fundamental decisions where to build houses and buildings and to which codes. At the very least, there are natural hazards. Nonetheless, with the advent of global warming and fracking, essentially all crises and disasters are now human-caused. Unfortunately, many organizations and industries have trouble acknowledging this.

Early Warning Signals

Next, my colleagues and I learned how crises unfold over time. Virtually, all crises are preceded by a long trail of early warning signals announcing the probable if not imminent occurrence of a crisis or a series of them. If an organization can pick up and act on these signals, then many crises can be prevented before they happen, the best form of crisis prevention, and thus, CM. The trouble is that there is a tremendous amount of noise in organizations that block important signals from getting to the right persons at the right times.

Even worse, very early on we discovered that many people, and thus organizations, don't want to know about the possibility of crises. If they acknowledged their possibility, then they'd have to do something about them that they are reluctant or don't know what to do. In far too many cases, crises are regarded as a personal failure for which people are blamed. Or at least this is the situation in crisis-prone organizations that are more susceptible to crises precisely because they downplay their vulnerabilities. In contrast, proactive crisis-prepared organizations reward people for pointing out potential crises and instituting programs of mitigation. As a result, we were not surprised to find that proactive crisis-prepared organizations were significantly more profitable than reactive crisis-prone ones. Proactive crisis-prepared organizations sought out and fixed problems before they turned into crises that could impact them and their surrounding communities. In brief, proactive organizations prepared for more crises than the ones they experienced.

In contrast, reactive organizations experienced more crises than the few for which they were prepared.

Because of the immense hold that The Technological Mindset has on its proponents, I doubt seriously that the tech industry will regard the fact that the UK has already passed laws to protect children from the worst excesses of the Internet as a strong early warning signal that the same could happen in the USA. It should also be taken seriously as an early warning signal of the potential backlash against technology in general. Indeed, there are clear signs that such a backlash is already brewing as the result of Facebook's most recent crisis.

Organizational Defense Mechanisms

The biggest breakthrough occurred because of my background in psychoanalytic thinking (once again the importance of Freud and Melanie Klein). My colleagues and I discovered that there were direct organizational counterparts to every one of the classic defense mechanisms first discovered by Sigmund Freud. Thus, the out-and-out denial of traumatic and unpleasant events took the organizational form of "We don't have any problems." Disavowal took the form of "All of our problems are minor." Compartmentalization took the form "Our problems are isolated and cannot bring down the entire system." Projection took the form that "Someone else, namely the competition, is to blame for our crises; or, someone is out to get us." Grandiosity took the form, "We're so big and powerful that nothing can bring us down." Idealization and Intellectualization took the form, "Excellent organizations don't have crises." That is, only "bad organizations" have crises. Splitting is thereby a major part of all crises.

The point is that no single discipline has a monopoly on how we need to think about complex, messy systems. Psychoanalytic thinking is every bit as fundamental as engineering and finance.

Every one of the components of The Technological Mindset discussed in Chapter 9 not only contains, but is a direct expression of Defense Mechanisms. For example, the contentions that "technology is the solution to all of our problems" and "technology is the single most important factor responsible for material and economic progress" are prime examples of Compartmentalization, Denial, Disavowal, Grandiosity, and Intellectualization. By choosing to see only the positive benefits of technology, and ignoring the negatives, The Technological Mindset thereby systematically not only denies, but downplays the potential crises produced by technology.

Crisis Audits

Different stakeholders also have different definitions as to what constitutes a crisis for them and their organization. Problem negotiation is thereby a vital part of CM. This led directly to the concept of crisis audits.

To find out the extent of the crises to which an organization was susceptible, my colleagues and I typically interviewed some 20–30 people. This included all of the top officers, a sampling of middle managers, as well as workers at the very bottom of an organization. The reason is as follows.

By virtue of their training and positions, Chief Financial Officers (CFOs) tend mainly to see financial crises; Heads of PR tend to see mainly PR and informational crises; Heads of Security, security crises; Heads of Legal, legal crises; Heads of Information Technology (IT), computer network crises, etc. Virtually, no one, not even the CEO, sees all the different crises to which an organization is susceptible. Often, those at the bottom have a more accurate and complete picture than those at the top. Hence, the importance of conducting interviews up and down is the hierarchy of an organization.

As a result of conducting audits with many different organizations in both the same and different industries, we were able to compile a robust list of the different types of possible crises. As a result, we were able to ask everyone we interviewed if they had thought about the possibility of the full range of different crises we identified. More often, they had not.

In presenting the summaries of our findings, generally to the top executives of an organization, we were able to show what they had and had not considered. As we studied more and more organizations in different industries, we were able to show comparable organizations that had experienced the types of crises that the organization for which we had conducted the audit had not considered at all, and in many cases, denied vehemently that they could ever happen to them.

Although we knew the general types of different crises, we couldn't necessarily know the particular forms that they could take in a specific organization. For this reason, worst-case scenarios became an integral part of crisis audits. That is, what are the worst ways in which a crisis thought to be improbable, if not impossible, could happen to an organization?

To be sure, conducting crisis audits of technological crises involves a range of different stakeholders that are not typically found within the confines of any single organization, e.g., academics, funders, competitors, and thought leaders. They are thus inherently political, but then, crisis audits are also highly political within any organization as well. Politics is not the death knell of crisis audits. By definition, virtually everything of importance in an organization or a group of people has a strong political element.

Proactive Crisis-Prepared Versus Reactive Organizations

To emphasize an earlier point, we discovered that proactive crisis-prepared organizations were significantly more profitable than reactive organizations. As I said before, the basic reason is proactive organizations basically prepared for more crises than they experienced, while reactive organizations experienced more crises than the few for which they were prepared. Thus, an organization's mind-set or culture was key. In a word, being proactive was not only the right, ethical thing to do, but it was good for business. It allowed one to head off crises before they became catastrophic and irreversible. As a result, crisis audits became an important component of quality control.

An Existential Definition of a Crisis

We also discovered a very different definition of a crisis based upon what crises do emotionally to people and organizations (NF, SF). True, a major crisis has the all-too-real potential to cause deaths, severe injuries, enormous destruction, significant drop in profits, loss in the value of a company's stock, bad publicity, major lawsuits, loss of trust, etc. (ST, NT). In addition, a major crisis does something even more insidious. It causes all of the important assumptions why a person or an organization thinks it won't ever have a crisis to crash, in short, to become invalid all at once. That's precisely why every crisis is an existential crisis of meaning (NF and SF). How does one continue to function if the rug is literally pulled out from under all of one's basic beliefs, and not just one or two, but all of them simultaneously?

Damage Containment Mechanisms

We also discovered the different forms and types of damage containment mechanisms, especially what worked and didn't. Damage containment mechanisms are critical because even with the best of preparations, crises are inevitable. Even though proactive CM prepared organizations experience substantially fewer crises than reactive crisis-prone organizations, proactive CM prepared organizations still experience them. In other words, no individual or organization is immune.

Essentially, there are seven major types of damage containment mechanisms:

1. Deflection
2. Stonewalling, i.e., Denial

3. Downplaying, i.e., Disavowal
4. Physical Containment
5. Dilution
6. Dispersion
7. Acknowledgment and Accepting Responsibility.

Deflection occurs when a person or organization that is primarily responsible for a crisis tries to deflect responsibility onto somebody or something else. Deflection almost always fails because in today's media-driven world, it's virtually impossible to hide anything about a person, organization, or whole society. With the loss of privacy across the board, for good and bad, there are no well-kept secrets any longer. In most cases, Deflection just makes the original crisis worse. If the initial crisis weren't bad enough, then attempts to cover it up only make it worse.

The same is true of Stonewalling and Denial. It's also true of Downplaying and Disavowal.

Physical Containment is exactly what its name implies. Here, attempts are made to keep a crisis confined within particular spaces and times where it can be contained. While this is obviously necessary in the case of fires and oil spills, it doesn't work well with other types of crises such as ethical ones.

While Dilution and Dispersion may also work well in the case of physical crises, e.g., treating oil spills with chemical dispersants or neutralizers, they do not work well in the case of ethical and social crises.

Of all the types, Acknowledgment and the Acceptance of Responsibility are not only the best, but often the only reasonable alternatives to save an individual, organization, and society. But it's also the most difficult and risky to undertake for it raises all-too-real possibility that everything relating to an individual or organization will be revealed. But then, crisis or not, the revelation of one's deepest secrets is virtually guaranteed in today's overly exposed and scrutinized world.

One of the key things about damage containment mechanisms is that they can't be invented in the "heat of battle," i.e., an actual crisis. A crisis is the worst time to practice proactive CM. If CM is not an integral part of an organization's everyday operations and culture, then it won't be easily performed, if at all, in an actual crisis, let alone in a series of crises. A case in point is Facebook's poor attempt to practice damage containment after the fact without prior preparation.

The premier example of the failure to invent damage containment mechanisms, have them well tested, and thus operational is BP's oil spill in the Gulf of Mexico. It took over a month to cap the wells. By then, millions of gallons of oil had spilled contaminating everything in its wake.

Prime Challenges in Creating New Fields

This brief review of CM illustrates some of the prime features and challenges in creating any new field. Definitions are obviously crucial (ST), but securing definitions is only part of understanding the basic nature of the fundamental phenomenon. In short, one needs a systemic understanding of the phenomenon (NT and NF).

It's also important to note that my understanding of CM was not achieved through academic studies alone and by staying within the strict confines of the university, i.e., physical isolation. When I was at USC, I founded and ran for ten years the USC Center for CM—one of the world's very first centers for CM. Corporate sponsors provided the basic funds so that we could do our research. But even more important, they gave us access to their organizations so we could see directly how they prepared for and experienced major crises. Once again, knowledge and its application cannot be separated.

Crises Due to Technology and the Technological Mindset

We are finally in a position to discuss the crises due to technology, and more specifically, The Technological Mindset.

Five major kinds of crises are especially germane to the technological revolution we are experiencing:

1. Loss of Meaning
2. Deceptiveness
3. Invasiveness
4. Decline in Relationships
5. Economic Displacement.

Needless to say, all five overlap significantly. They are in fact parts of a wicked mess.

Crises of meaning refer to the loss of dignity, hope, meaning, self-esteem, and a sense of purpose as a result of by being replaced by technology. I don't mean only the natural and inevitable feelings of anxiety despair due to the loss of a job, but also the overpowering feeling that one is obsolete and thereby ultimately worthless. It's a human crisis of immense proportions. Once again, those who stand to profit richly from any technology that threatens to displace "large numbers of workers" must be held accountable. They must be required to set up funds for the retraining of workers. Further, the phrase "large numbers of workers" must be interpreted carefully lest it leads to an unacceptable ethical threshold, for one displaced worker is one too many.

Crises of Deception refer to when only the positive aspects/impacts of a technology are presented to the public and the negative aspects/impacts are intentionally hidden from view, downplayed, or ignored altogether. When the negatives occur, as they eventually must, feelings of deep betrayal become predominant. It also occurs when people are deceived as to how their personal data will be used. A backlash against technology is the inevitable result.

Crisis audits must thereby be a fundamental part of the development of any technology. If the negative effects threaten to cause irreversible harm that are unpreventable, then a technology must not be allowed to proceed. Proactive CM must be given top priority. The best form of damage containment is crisis prevention.

Crises of Invasiveness occur when technology intervenes so deeply in our brains, bodies, social institutions, etc., such that we feel we are no longer human. The same cautions and protections apply as before.

Crises of Relationships occur when technology alters for the worse how we relate to one another, the environment, fellow creatures, etc.

Social media need to undertake continuous, frequent Public Service Announcements (PSAs) urging children to put their phones to bed at appropriate times.

In this regard, parents have reported the undermining of their authority when Siri and its Amazon counterpart have said one thing to their children and the parents have said another, e.g., whether to wear a raincoat or not.[1]

Crises of Economic Displacement result when our lives are upended due to being replaced by technology. The same precautions apply as before.

As parts of a wicked mess, the different types are highly interactive. This leads to the most far-reaching proposal of all. There needs to be some societal mechanism—a body—that not only monitors individual technologies, but especially investigates how they interact both positively and negatively. I know of no societal body at present that undertakes this crucial function.

More Specific Types

In response to the more general types of crises described in the preceding section, it's also possible to list more specific crises to which technology companies are especially vulnerable.

1. Boycotts
2. Protests
3. Negative Publicity
4. Environmental Harm and Destruction Caused by Basic Products and Services
5. The Abuse and Misuse of Basic Products and Services
6. Failure to Disclose/Warn About Potential Disbenefits and Negative Attributes of Basic Products and Services
7. How Positive Attributes/Properties Can Become Negatives.

There are of course more than just these seven, but they are more than sufficient to form the basis of a crisis audit of any organization.

Again, each and every one is capable of triggering all of the others. Systems Thinking is key.

Risk Management (RM)

Since so many organizations practice RM, it's important to discuss so that we can contrast and compare it to CM.

RM rests on the following core ideas. Suppose one has an unbiased coin. If one tosses it one hundred times, one would expect it on average to come up heads 50 times and tails 50 times. (Actually, an unbiased coin can come up any amount of heads and tails as long as they add up to one hundred.) Suppose further that every time the coin comes up heads one wins a dollar and every time it comes up tails, one loses two dollars. On average, one would expect to get 50 times one dollar minus 50 times two dollars or to lose 50 dollars. That is, $50 \times \$1 - 50 \times \$2 = -\$50$.

In more general terms, the number of times or probability that heads comes up multiplied by the amount of money one gets or loses if a head shows plus the number of times or probability that tails comes up multiplied by the amount of money one gets or loses if a tail comes up equals on average the total amount of money one expects to make or to lose. In the theory of probability, this procedure is known as Expected Value, i.e., the amount of money we expect to make or lose on average. Accordingly, Risk is equal to Expected Value. In the worst case, it equals the number of expected injuries, deaths, etc.

Unfortunately, the problems with this seemingly simple procedure are not only many, but often quite serious. Even if one has a lot of historical data, one rarely knows exactly or reliably the probabilities that something will fail or succeed today or tomorrow. To extrapolate from past historical records, one has to make the critical assumption that the future will be like the past. One also has to make the critical assumption (argument) that the conditions that made for past performance will be the same for future performance. This requires that one knows or assumes what past conditions were. Even if these conditions are known, they can still change, often drastically and suddenly, without one necessarily being aware of them.

The procedure also assumes that we know what the consequences of failure or success are. For many situations, we don't know or have such knowledge.

The procedure is also flawed in the sense that we never experience the "expected" or "average" costs of success and failure. We experience the "actual" costs. That is, we don't necessarily experience the costs or benefits in terms of the procedure for calculating Risks. Thus, if a $1,500,000 house burns down, then more likely than not, it will cost much more than $1,500,000 to rebuild it to today's standards. And, we don't necessarily experience the "average cost" associated with replacing hundreds of houses.

The same problems arise if instead of using data, we use mathematical models for estimating probabilities or consequences. For this and other reasons, I am extremely dubious with regard to the typical applications of RM. This doesn't mean that I never calculate Risks, but that I calculate and use them very differently.

For instance, in working with organizations, my colleagues and I typically split a group of 16–20 people into four subgroups. One group is asked to consider the assumptions they have to make, for example, that a disaster hitting their city or town is both highly probable and high in costs. Another is asked to consider the assumptions they have to make such that a disaster hitting their location is low in probability, but high in costs. Still another is asked to consider the assumptions they have to make that a disaster is highly probable, but low in costs. Finally, the last group is asked to consider the assumptions they have to make such that a disaster is low in probability and low in costs.

The reason for having four groups explicitly look at the same event from four different perspectives is that the assumptions underlying the use of RM are too critical to trust a single number that purports to represent "'the true Risks' associated with a critical situation." I am extremely reluctant to trust any single number that purports to measure Risk (ST). For the same reason that one cannot trust any single person to identify all the possible crises that can happen to an organization without knowing the assumptions that led to it. In a word, one cannot trust any single number to represent the true Risks facing an organization.

This is precisely why in working with organizations to help them improve their RM procedures, my colleagues and I recommend that at least two different teams with two very different perspectives identify and score Risks (NT, NF). Yes, this costs more than just having one team, but it also helps to lower the costs of not identifying and preparing for a crisis that one later regrets. As they become more practiced, an organization can have just one team that looks at two very different scenarios.

There is another aspect of RM that is equally troubling. Since Risks are determined by multiplying the probability of the occurrence of an event by its consequences measured either in dollars, lives lost, injuries, etc., a cut-off point is usually specified in comparing multiple Risks. Risks are thereby ranked in terms of their Expected Value and those that are below a certain cut-off level or threshold are typically ignored. This means that disasters such as 9/11 that are very low in probability but high in consequences are often ignored. In sharp contrast, CM does not ignore such Risks. CM considers potential crises irrespective of their probabilities of occurrence. *At least one of the each of the different types of crises must be included as basic components of an organization's Crisis Portfolio.* This is precisely why I am such a staunch advocate of CM. And, this is precisely what proactive crisis-prepared organizations do. They connect individual crises. They think and act systemically.

There is another equally troubling aspect of RM. Calculating Risks without plans for managing them is at best only half of the task. What good is it to know the magnitude of Risks if we have no way of managing them before, during, and after their occurrence, assuming of course that we have calculated the probabilities and magnitudes of the Risk accurately to begin with?

If RM has such serious problems, why then is it used so widely? RM appeals to a high-tech society such as ours that is highly enamored of science and technology. For all its faults and limitations, RM confers the patina of precision, exactitude, and most of all, "Hard Science." RM is thus used to help protect organizations legally and politically. They claim that they have used the best tools currently available to protect themselves and the public from widespread harm. But RM is anything but a "Hard Science." It is dependent upon countless assumptions, many of which we are not aware.

As an important aside, NO science is ever completely "hard." Every science rests on a bedrock of critical, taken-for-granted assumptions. In terms of the earlier discussion of "hard" versus "soft" fields of study, I deliberately refrain from calling such assumptions "soft," as far too many unfortunately do, because calling something "soft" demeans its importance. One of the most critical assumptions underlying RM is that it can be applied to complex situations. The concept of Expected Value, which underlies RM, was developed historically for relatively simple situations such as the tossing of coins, dice, and drawing of cards. These situations are bounded and well structured enough such that the probabilities and consequences of various events such as getting 50 heads in a row or drawing an ace from a deck of cards can be computed. But without positing some very strong assumptions, it does not follow that the concept of Expected Value can be applied wholesale to complex situations.

If one uses the notion of drawing of cards from a deck as a basic metaphor for RM, then a better idea is that we are not dealing with a fixed deck of cards with constant face values. Instead, every time we draw a card, the number of cards in the deck changes in some unpredictable fashion and the face values of the cards also change unpredictably as well. This better reflects the true realities with which we are dealing.

Even if we were able to measure Risks accurately and reliably, by itself this does not necessarily help us to manage them because the act of measurement does not automatically lead to good management. The Great Financial Recession of 2008 demonstrated that a number of the banks that were deemed "Too Large to Fail" told their RM departments in effect to "take a hike." The money that was being made in risky transactions was far too much to be hamstrung by overzealous considerations of Risk even though the estimates of Risk were close to the mark in many instances.

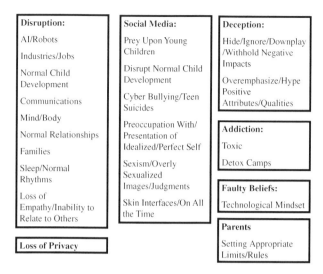

Fig. 11.1 Full array of crises

Concluding Remarks

Unfortunately, when it comes to technology, for the most part, society is content to adopt a reactive approach to CM. Instead of thinking seriously about and mitigating the negative and most dangerous aspects of technologies, we mainly opt for cleaning them up later, if then. We can no longer continue to operate in this way.

Finally, without further comment, Fig. 11.1 gives the full array of crises with which technology is associated, if not responsible for.

Postscript: Thinking About the Unthinkable

There is little doubt that thinking about the unthinkable poses one of the greatest challenges of all. How does one go thinking about the crises that have never struck one's organization or industry? Little wonder why far too many people and organizations just throw up their hands and say that it's just impossible. And yet, it's not.

Since 2006, I've been a member of the Center for Catastrophic Risk Management (CCRM) at UC Berkeley, my alma mater. During that time, we've witnessed scores of presentations from all types of organizations in different industries. In reviewing the power points that accompany the presentations, one thing stands out. All of the organizations are relatively well prepared for core crises and threats that they face regularly. Thus, the oil and chemical industries don't have to be prodded to prepare for fires and explosions for they come with the basic territory. Nonetheless, they have to be prodded to prepare for crises and threats that are seemingly outside of their everyday experience. Thus, for instance, product tampering is not typically on their "radar screens." That is, it isn't until one reminds them that the gas stations that they own and operate have mini-marts that sell food and other products such as pain medication. Then, product tampering becomes an all-too-real possibility.

My experience with CCRM has taught me that the best, if not the only way, of thinking about the unthinkable is to expose organizations to the crises and threats that other organizations in other industries face regularly. Instead of dismissing such crises and threats outright, organizations then need to be encouraged to go through worst-case scenarios that force them to consider, "How could such and such crises or threats happen to us?" While such an exercise is far from perfect, it's a viable way of thinking about the unthinkable.

Post-Postscript: Facebook, the Epitome of a Crisis-Prone Company

One of the key findings of my research and consulting bears emphasizing: Unfortunately, there is a class of organizations that are crisis-prone. Crisis-prone companies don't just experience one or two isolated crises, but they lurch almost uncontrollably from one crisis to the next again and again. In short, they are unable to get out in front, learn from their own crises and those of others, so that they can anticipate and prevent new crises from happening.

Facebook fits the definition and profile of a crisis-prone company. Whether it realizes it or not—and it's obvious that it doesn't really comprehend it—it's at a real crossroads. It needs to be reconstituted from top to bottom. Its business and operating model are extremely flawed. Indeed, recently the CEO of Salesforce has called for Facebook to be regulated like cigarette companies because of the addictive effects of its product on kids. And, for essentially the same reasons, Tim Cook, Apple's CEO, has said that he wouldn't let children use social media.

Consider the following list of crises for which Facebook is responsible:

1. Cyber bulling:
   Since Facebook is available 24/7/365, many kids report being harassed and hounded relentlessly at all hours of the days and nights with never a letup; though rare, suicides have occurred;
2. The Use of Face Recognition Technology to Prey Upon the Most Vulnerable Teens and Young Children[2]:
   As I noted previously, despicably, Facebook has used Face Recognition Technology to monitor the emotions of young users; it's then sold the information associated with those who exhibit noticeable anxieties to third parties who prey on the kids to sell them stuff that panders to their insecurities;
3. The Interference in the 2016 Presidential Election by Foreign Parties, namely Russia:
   According to multiple U.S. Intelligence Agencies, Russia used Facebook as a major platform to disseminate dis- and misinformation designed explicitly to alter the outcome of the 2016 U.S. presidential election;
4. Salacious Ads/Fake News:
   Facebook has also allowed itself to be used as a major platform for the dissemination of salacious ads and Fake News;
5. Heightened Threats to the Mental Health of Young Children:
   According to multiple researchers, those children and young adults who are heavy users of Facebook are significantly more prone to higher rates of depression, lower self-esteem, more frequent and severe anxiety attacks, etc. In other words, the more one uses Facebook, the more one's mental health is at risk;

6. A Recent Major Segment on NBC by Former Facebook Employees and Funders Accusing It of Putting Profits Over the Well-Being of Users:

In the direct words of one of the persons on the segment, "Facebook is a crime scene." It ignored repeatedly clear and persistent signals that things were amiss, i.e., that major crises of its own making were highly likely.

In the same vein, it's also been accused of feeding the anger and raising anxieties of its users in order to increase "traffic" to its site;

That may be "good business" for Facebook, but not for the health and well-being of society as a whole where trust in all institutions is already at all-time lows;

7. Time and Time Again, Prodded into Taking Action:

One of the major characteristics of crisis-prone companies is that they are reactive when it comes to taking preventive actions.

Only when the howls of protest have become so great and prolonged has Facebook finally been prodded into doing what it should have been doing all along. To emphasize an earlier point, there are no good reasons why prior to its launch, teams of parents, teachers, psychologists, and kids themselves couldn't have come up with the idea that Facebook could be a perfect vehicle for cyberbullying. I cannot emphasize enough that all technologies are used and abused in ways that their creators don't want to think about; and

8. And of course, at the time of this writing, its worse crisis of all:

The authorized release of the personal data of 87 million of its users. In a word, Facebook has violated the most basic commodity any business has, the trust of its users.

Notes

1. Tanith Carey, "Hey Alexa, What Are You Teaching My Children?," *The Telegraph*, April 6, 2018.
2. Paul Armstrong, "Facebook Is Helping Brands Target Teens Who Feel Helpless," *Forbes*, May 1, 2017.

12

Inquiry Systems, William James, John Dewey, Edward Singer, C. West Churchman

The following quotes by Jonathan Mahler and Tom Nichols capture some of the pertinent themes of the chapter:

> …somewhere along the way, the democratization of the flow of information became the democratization of the flow of disinformation. The distinction between fact and fiction was erased, creating a sprawling universe of competing claims…[1]

> …Americans have reached the point where ignorance—at least regarding what is generally considered established knowledge in public policy—is seen as an actual virtue. To reject the advice of experts is to assert autonomy, a way for Americans to demonstrate their independence from nefarious elites—and insulate their increasingly fragile egos from ever being told they're wrong.[2]

In Chapter 6, I touched on one of the most important topics of this book, Inquiry Systems. They are the foundations for knowledge, if not reasoned thought itself. As such, they underlie every human activity.

Portions of Chapter Twelve are reprinted with permission of Stanford University Press.

© The Author(s) 2019
I. I. Mitroff, *Technology Run Amok*,
https://doi.org/10.1007/978-3-319-95741-8_12

They are also the foundations for thinking about, and hence coping with, wicked messes. For this reason, I want to present an overview of five basic kinds of Inquiry Systems that are integral to Western thought. One of the benefits of the discussion is that it allows us to see that Fake News is a perverse form of inquiry. Indeed, in terms of the Toulmin Argumentation Framework, the assertion that something is fake is often nothing more than the assertion of a Claim without any Evidence to back it up.

Unfortunately, despite the fact that the history of Western thought has shown that other systems of inquiry are better suited for complex, messy problems, two particular Inquiry Systems are dominant. They not only underlie Western education and science, but as such, they are largely taken-for-granted. The result is that they are not seriously challenged or questioned as much as they should be. Not only is it assumed implicitly that they are generally applicable to all problems, but that they are the only Inquiry Systems for general use. This is especially unfortunate because others are actually more appropriate for wicked messes.

Inquiry Systems

Inquiry Systems are not only particular ways of obtaining knowledge, but even more, they differ fundamentally with respect to what they label worthy of the term "knowledge." In a word, they have very different conceptions of "knowledge and truth." In effect, each Inquiry System represents a different philosophical method and school for obtaining knowledge, indeed what it recognizes as knowledge in the first place.[3]

A Prosaic Example

In order to make a complex topic as accessible as possible, I want to use the example of a fictitious company, Healthy Bars, Inc.

As its name implies, Healthy Bars Inc. makes healthy food energy bars. Its goal is not only to be the number one company in its industry in terms of market share, but it wants to be the company that consumers think of first when they think of an environmentally responsible, ethical company.

In order to increase awareness of its products so that it could boost sales, Healthy Bars Inc. decided to hold a worldwide contest. They invited consumers to send in recipes on "how to make the perfect fruit bar."[4] The only restriction was that the recipes had to use one of Healthy Bars Inc.'s products. Other than this, consumers were free to add any ingredients they wished, providing of course that they were safe, environmentally friendly, and legal. The contest winner not only received free health bars for a year, but more importantly, the honorific title of "master chef."

The First Way of Deciding: Expert Consensus

Like most organizations, Healthy Bars Inc. appointed a small committee to judge the entries it received. To its chagrin, the committee soon found that it was literally drowning in thousands of entries that poured in from all over the world. As a result, the committee was completely stymied. There was no way that a small group could sift through thousands of submissions.

Besides, what was the meaning of "perfect?" They hadn't considered that a definition of what they were looking for would be important before they started the contest. Rather naively, they thought that a definition would just emerge, if they even considered it important to contemplate at all.

It's only in bounded, well-defined, and well-structured problems—in other words ST exercises—where everything is either "given" or known beforehand that we start with a clear definition of what the problem is at the very beginning of an inquiry. Furthermore, the initial definition of the problem does not vary over the course of the study. This is definitely not true of unbounded, ill-structured problems where the problem or problems only become fully known, if then, as an inquiry unfolds. It's also not true of other Inquiry Systems, which start with the presumption that the world is composed of complex, messy problems, not simple well-defined exercises.

For instance, "$x + 6 + 11$, find x" is an exercise and not a problem in the true sense of the term. First of all, everything is "given," i.e., well defined for the student. Second, everyone is expected to get the single right answer $x = 5$. Real problems have none of these characteristics. In principle, each stakeholder is more likely than not to have a very different definition of the problem and hence seek a very different solution.

Thus, if Sandra is a single mother of two and only has $2500 for the entire month to feed and clothe herself and her children, plus pay rent, but she needs a minimum of $3000, that's a real problem. The "solution" is certainly not just the numerical difference between $3000 and $2500, but how Sandra can receive the help she needs to survive.

To continue with the example of Healthy Bars, one of the committee members suggested tabulating all the entries by putting them into a PC. The particular recipe receiving the most votes or the one that had the most in common with all the individual recipes—the "average"—would be declared the winner, in this case, the "perfect fruit bar." The member pointed out that this was a convenient way of bypassing the definition of "perfect." "Perfect" would in effect emerge from the process itself. As one of the committee members said, "Why get hung up on definitions?"

However, as soon as this was suggested, it raised more concerns and issues than it settled. Most of the members felt that it was a complete copout.

Why was the "average," or the recipe receiving the most votes, in any way the definition of "perfect?" Wouldn't it lead to the selection of the most bland and inoffensive entry? Besides, what did it mean to "average" entries from around the world? Were all entries equal? Was everyone who submitted an entry automatically an "expert?" Were all experts equal? To believe so may be "democratic" and "anti-elitist," but was it best suited to the task at hand?

In effect, <u>the committee couldn't agree among themselves to use the Method of Agreement to settle the contest!</u> This particular method was thus rejected before it even got started. The taken-for-granted, implicit assumption that the problem was bounded and well structured was false, and therefore, strongly overruled.

Even if they polled "recognized experts" for their opinions, there would still be problems. For instance, how would they define an expert? If "recognized experts" were defined as the "community" of "distinguished chefs" worldwide, say all those working in Michelin two-star restaurants or better, the committee still felt that this way of choosing the winner would be inadequate, for it would privilege a certain group of "experts" over others.

In using experts, one is not only dependent on the consensus between them for producing "truth" in the first place—in this case "'truth' is the 'perfect' fruit bar"—but one is also assuming that the more agreement there is between experts, the stronger, and therefore, the "better" the "resultant truth."[5] In this system, "truth" is that with which a group of experts agrees strongly.

Appropriately enough, this approach is known as The Expert Consensus Way of Knowing or of Producing Knowledge. "Truth" is both the product of and the outcome of the agreement between the independent judgments, observations, or opinions of different experts. For brevity, I refer to it as Expert Agreement or Expert Consensus.

Again, consider global warming. The "body of 'reputable scientists worldwide'" is now in strong, if not overwhelming, agreement that human activities are mainly responsible for global warming. This "fact" which is based on enumerable scientific studies is taken as "strong Evidence" that the debate whether humans are or are not responsible for global warming is essentially over, even if all the mechanisms for it are not completely understood at the present.

More often than not, this Inquiry System forces agreement as much as it produces it. Therefore, unless one knows how agreement was produced—whether it was arrived at freely or not—then it's exceedingly misleading and even dangerous to trust it.

The Second Way of Deciding: "The One True Formula!"

One of the members on the committee had a B.S. in chemistry from a top university. She argued that chemistry should be used to derive the ingredients and the recipe for the perfect fruit bar. The winner of the contest would be that person or persons whose submission matched the recipe derived from this procedure.

In the second system or model of inquiry, the perfect recipe is based on the theoretical principles and laws of some "hard science" such as chemistry, and that particular science alone. In this system, there is a direct link with science. Science is in fact _the model_ for inquiry. "Truth" is equivalent to an algorithm or formula.

The reasoning is that "the perfect fruit bar"—truth itself—should not be based on anything so crass as the mere opinions of a group of experts no matter how distinguished they may be. Truth shouldn't even be based on what a particular set of experts regard as the "facts" because the "facts" of one group and age have an uncanny way of becoming the falsehoods of another. After all, that the Earth was flat was a widely accepted "fact" for hundreds if not thousands of years.

Truth "should" be based on the established principles—laws— of hard science. (Notice that use of the word "should" means that this system, as all systems do, rests on a prime ethical commitment.) Proceeding from firmly established scientific first principles, one should be able to derive a single formula. Recall that in the case of a falling body, the distance D that it covers in a certain amount of time T is given by the formula, $D = (1/2)\ G\ T^2$ where G equals the acceleration due to gravity. Since the formula D for falling bodies can be derived directly from Newton's law of gravitation—one of the first principles of physical science—the formula is akin to a "hard law of Nature." That is, if one knows the differential and integral calculus, then D can be derived from Newton's law of gravitation. The important point is that this system seeks to produce a single abstract formula that it regards as "the truth."

Appropriately enough, this system is known as the Pure Theory Way of Knowing. For short, I refer to it as The One True Formula.

This system is actually much broader than mathematics or science alone. Much more basic is the idea that the Pure Theory Way of Knowing is a coherent belief system—a framework of basic, presumably rational, first principles that are internally consistent. It cannot be the case that an assertion or proposition and its negation are both true at the same time. In this broader sense, this system does not always appear in the form of a formula. Recall the discussion of The Technological Mindset, which is as strong an example of this form of inquiry as one could hope to find.

Needless to say, the committee didn't buy this way of choosing the winner as well. Why should the winner be decided by a single scientific discipline, let alone something so ridiculous as a single formula? Why was chemistry superior to any other science, or for that matter, any non-scientific discipline or profession such as "culinary science?"

If one was restricted to choosing a single discipline, why shouldn't it be psychology? Weren't the attitudes of the contestants just as important as the physical ingredients themselves?

Since based on their own first principles the committee couldn't answer their specific questions, they rejected the method of First Principles in choosing the winner.

The Third Way: Multiple Perspectives, Multiple Formulas

One of the committee members suggested an approach with which all of the members agreed instantly. For the first time, they felt that they were making headway.

Notice that in agreeing so readily, they were buying into the first method, Expert Agreement. In effect, they were using the first way of producing knowledge to select another way of producing it.[6] There is nothing inherently wrong with combining Inquiry Systems. This is in fact an important way of getting around the weaknesses of any single system. "Truth" no longer depends upon a single system. Of course, by itself, this does not make the "truths" produced by this or any other Inquiry System necessarily superior.

Instead of lumping all of the entries together and averaging them suppose that one grouped them initially by countries or regions of the world. Or, suppose that one first grouped them by different schools or philosophies of cooking. Then, from each group, one could select a winner by using the first way of knowing, i.e., Expert Consensus.[7]

Instead of their being a single, best formula for all of the entries, suppose that each group of entries had its own special formula. Using each formula, one would determine the winners of each group, and from these, one could if possible select an overall winner.

The third system is a combination of the first two: Expert Agreement and The One True Formula. In this approach, backed up by whatever data and facts they have to support their judgments, one samples the opinions of different regions or schools of cooking. Presumably, each region or school has its own distinct recipe or formula.

This system allows a decision-maker to witness explicitly how the outcome, the perfect fruit bar, varies as one changes the underlying method or formula (recipe) for producing it. It thus allows a decision-maker, in this case, the committee, who may not be an expert, or a proponent of, any particular school of cooking, to better understand the reasoning behind each school by seeing how they each approach the "same problem."

This system allows one to see explicitly the differences between various approaches. In other words, it does not leave variety to chance. Unlike the first two ways, this Inquiry System does not believe that there is one and only one best answer to complex problems or questions.

The third way believes that on any problem of importance, one must produce *at least two* different views of the problem. Unless we have two or more different formulations of a problem, we cannot possibly know whether we are attempting to solve the "wrong" or the "right" problem. And in fact, without two or more views to compare, the terms "right" and "wrong" have no meaning, unless of course one has very good reasons for believing unequivocally in the "truth" of a single system or way of looking at the world. This system is thus a minimal requirement for ascertaining whether we are committing Type Three Errors, solving the wrong problems precisely.

The third way of knowing is the basis of critical thinking. It forces one to examine the assumptions that underlie any particular formulation of a problem by explicitly comparing different formulations. After one has witnessed the differences between different approaches, one can, if it's possible, and one wishes, pick and choose—blend if need be—between them to form one's own unique recipe.

Appropriately enough, this system is known as the Multiple Perspective or the Multiple Formula Approach to Knowledge. It argues that complex problems are too important to be left to the reasoning of any single approach no matter how appealing it is. Indeed, the more that a particular approach is appealing, the more one needs to resist the temptation to fall under its sway.

This system is also the basis of multidisciplinary inquiry. The end result is a conclusion or recommendation that is the product of two or more scientific disciplines or professions. But since the disciplines or professions that are involved in multidisciplinary inquiry are not affected by one another—they remain separate and distinct—this system is not interdisciplinary. The basic disciplines and the professions themselves do not change as a result of their being involved in the third way of knowing. We have to reach the level of the fifth system, Systems Thinking, before we can say that we are engaged in interdisciplinary inquiry.

In Systems Thinking, the various disciplines and professions interact so strongly such that they modify one another. At the very least, each discipline and profession depends fundamentally on at least one concept from all the other disciplines and professions.

Finally, there is another aspect of this system that is very important to note. The first two systems assume that data (expert judgments, facts, observations, etc.) and theory are independent of one another. Expert Agreement assumes that one can gather data, facts, and observations on an issue or phenomenon without having to presuppose any prior theory about the issue or phenomenon. It assumes that data, facts, and observations are theory and value-free.

In contrast, The One Best Formula assumes that theories are free or independent of data, facts, and observations. In principle, the formulation of theories is dependent only upon pure thought or logic alone.

The third system stresses that our prior beliefs, whether in the form of The One True Formula or not, affect what we decide is important to collect or to observe. Every observation we make presumes that we understand enough about the nature of the underlying phenomenon such that we know what's important to observe. This "decision," certainly the critical assumptions upon which it is based, is a form of "theory," however informal it may be. In this sense, every observation presupposes some prior theory. Data, facts, and observations are not theory-free. They certainly are not value-free given that we often have to allocate significant resources in money and time to collect any and all data.

The upshot is that ethics is an important part of every inquiry, whether we acknowledge it or not. In fact, the less we acknowledge it, the more that ethics is important because instead of examining and debating our ethical assumptions, the more we take them for granted.

Ethics is a key component because in choosing what to observe, certainly what data to collect, in effect we are saying what we "ought" to observe and/or collect.

Notice that there is no absolute guarantee that the different views will select the perfect fruit bar. Nonetheless, this Inquiry System assumes that there is even less of a guarantee if one uses one and only way of looking at a problem.

It's especially important to observe how this Inquiry System applies directly to crisis and risk management. The assessment of crises and risks is too important to be left to the determination of any single point of view. As I noted before, at a minimum, one requires two very different perspectives before one can trust the judgments as to what and what are not important crises and risks.

Finally, it's extremely important to point out that this system gives a very different interpretation of the vulgar phrase "alternate facts." It disputes the whole notion strongly. True, each of the different perspectives in multiple inquiry is not only compatible with, but leads to different facts, but this doesn't mean that anything goes or that all "facts" are thereby equal. It means that in order for there to be "facts" of any kind, one has to use appropriate theories to surface the "facts" that are compatible with a particular perspective or theory. Thus, the appraisal, let alone the acceptance of a set of "facts," is dependent upon our being able to examine and appraise the underlying theories that are responsible for the "facts," a "fact" that those disposed to "alternate facts" don't understand.

The Fourth Way: Expert Disagreement

Someone in the committee had another idea. Instead of depending upon the <u>agreement</u> between experts, suppose they used <u>disagreement</u>. The winner of the debate between experts would then be the winner of the contest.

The fourth approach is the direct opposite of the first. Whereas consensus is the guarantor of the perfect fruit bar, and the way to produce it (truth in general) in the first approach, intense conflict is the guarantor, and the way to obtain it, in the fourth model.

The guarantor is one of the most important and critical parts of Inquiry Systems. The guarantor is the part that "guarantees" that starting with the "right" initial building blocks of knowledge (basic assumptions, elemental or fundamental "truths," data, facts, observations, etc.) and combining them in the "right ways," e.g., averaging the responses, using various mathematical operations, differing arguments or modes of reasoning, then one will arrive at "the best estimate of the truth, if not Truth itself."

In the fourth approach, one picks two schools of cooking that are in the greatest opposition, and hence, disagree the most. This was in fact the basis for the clichéd TV program Iron Chef. One then arranges a knockdown, no holds barred, debate between them. The recipe that emerges from (survives) the debate, which may be neither of the original two recipes, is then dubbed the "truth." Appropriately, this model is known as The Dialectical Theory or Model of Knowledge. It is also known as The Conflict Theory of Truth, or Expert Disagreement for short.

Alfred P. Sloan

To show how the fourth approach applies to business, and therefore in essence to all professions, consider the following: Alfred P. Sloan, Chairman of General Motors from 1937 to 1956, was one of the very few executives who not only understood the importance of the fourth way, but used it regularly when he had an important decision to make. Of course, he didn't necessarily refer to it by the name of Expert Disagreement, let alone was conscious of it as a distinct and valid form of inquiry.

When his top executives agreed too readily with his ideas, Sloan is reputed to have said, "I propose we postpone further discussion until our next meeting to give ourselves time to develop disagreement and perhaps gain some understanding of what the decision is all about."[8]

If possible, this Inquiry System works by feeding the "same set of data" to both of the strongly opposing worldviews of a problem or situation. One then has the opportunity to witness explicitly how two diametrically opposed views interpret the "same data" in order to reach totally opposing conclusions. Notice carefully that some other initial theory or worldview about the situation is necessary in order to collect "the same data" that both of the contesting worldviews would then interpret differently.

For example, based on the same numbers of enemies versus Americans killed, Hawks and Doves reached totally opposing conclusions on the status of the Vietnam War. Hawks used the data to "prove" that the USA was winning the war while Doves used the same data to show that the USA was losing it.

The fundamental presumption of this Inquiry System is that far more than agreement, conflict will reveal the underlying assumptions of each worldview. It's also assumed that as a result of witnessing the debate, a decision-maker will be in a better position to form his or her own view of an important problem. Of course, this is not necessarily the case since many people are often confused and paralyzed by a debate, more generally, by conflict of any kind, let alone the kinds of intense conflict that is an integral feature of this system of inquiry. The point is that each Inquiry System appeals to a different underlying psychology. Along with ethics, psychology is thereby one of the most important components of every Inquiry System.

FDR Versus Eisenhower

One of the most important examples of Expert Disagreement is the following.

Very few people and organizations do what President Franklin Delano Roosevelt (FDR) did when he was faced with a difficult policy decision, which of course all Presidents face regularly. Unbeknownst to either one, FDR assigned two analysts to research a problem from two completely different and opposing perspectives. When both were finished, they were ushered into the Oval Office to make their reports in person and directly in front of one another. While the process was highly disconcerting to each analyst, FDR felt that he wasn't properly informed unless he witnessed explicitly and side-by-side at least two widely contesting views of an important issue. FDR believed that the only way he could begin to understand the assumptions that underlay every important issue was by having two analysts analyze it from two very different and opposing perspectives. Only then could FDR decide whether to go with either perspective or neither one. Frequently, he had the analysts go back and formulate a new option by integrating their original, diverse perspectives. Or, based on their opposing presentations, they came up with entirely new options.

Contrast this with the decision-making behavior of President Dwight David Eisenhower. When faced with a difficult issue, President Eisenhower just wanted the single recommendation with which his advisors agreed presented to him. Undoubtedly, this was due in large part to his many years in the military. In effect, he believed unequivocally in Expert Agreement or Consensus.

To repeat, the downfall of Expert Agreement is that it is only for very simple and extremely well-structured issues and problems—exercises—that one can generally trust without serious challenges and questions the agreement between different experts or policy advisors.

The Fifth Way: Systems Thinking

The committee still wasn't satisfied. They felt that something fundamentally was missing, but they didn't know exactly what it was. Someone finally exclaimed, "We need help."

With this, another person added, "We're thinking too narrowly. We need to expand our thinking." This led her to say, "Maybe we need to bring in someone who can help us to think more broadly. Isn't this what Systems Thinking is all about? Why don't we call in a systems expert?"

The last way of knowing is the most comprehensive of all, or at least that's its goal. It is known as the Systems Way of Thinking, or simply, Systems Thinking.

In this model, one sweeps in considerations that are typically overlooked in the first four models. (See Chapter 13 for a more extensive discussion of the meaning and rationale of "sweeping in.") For instance, ethical and aesthetic considerations are given center stage. Using the "right," i.e., "ethical," ingredients that are not harmful to the environment is central in this approach. For another, the ambience or the aesthetic design of the kitchen in which a fruit bar is produced is as important as the actual physical recipe itself. In fact, anything that affects the mental state and the well-being of the cook is potentially an essential part of the "recipe," for example, the lighting and the color of the walls of the kitchen, etc.

This helped to put some of the entries in a "special light." A few of the entries described the setting in which they prepared their submissions. They felt that the kitchen in which the fruit bars were prepared was as important as the raw ingredients themselves. For this reason, they included pictures of their kitchens along with their recipes.

The Essence of Systems Thinking

The last way of knowing is based on the work of C. West Churchman and his mentor E. A. Singer Jr.[9] In turn, Singer was one of the best students of the eminent American philosopher William James, a topic about which I say more in the next chapter.

Singer emphasized throughout his work that there are no "basic" or "fundamental disciplines." For Singer and Churchman, no science, no profession, or field of knowledge was more basic or superior to any other. This idea is so important that it is one of the fundamental cornerstones of Systems Thinking.

In Systems Thinking, the physical sciences, certainly knowledge about the physical world, are inseparable from the social sciences and knowledge about the social world. In Churchman's and Singer's philosophy, the physical and the social sciences are not only inseparable, but they presuppose one another. Neither is possible without the other. (In the same way that all of the four Myers-Briggs perspectives fundamentally depend on one another.)

Whether we admit it or not, physical science is done by all-too-real human beings that not only have a "psychology" but operate within a "social context." The psychology and the sociology of the investigator not only affect the production of physical knowledge, but its very existence.[10] My study of the Apollo Moon scientist's demonstrated this repeatedly.

Objectivity

The discussion of different Inquiry Systems helps to make clear why the frequent admonition to be "objective" is in most cases laughable if not meaningless. Which <u>kind</u> of objectivity is the proper response?

According to Expert Agreement, something is objective if and only if it is based on "hard data, facts, or observations" and the "tight agreement" between different observers as to the meaning of the data, etc.

According to the One True Formula, something is objective if and only if it is based on logical reasoning from self-evident first principles or premises. The trouble is that as the American humorist Ambrose Bierce observed, "self-evident means evident to one's self and to no one else."

According to Multiple Perspectives, something is objective if and only if it is the product and the result of multiple points of view.

According to Expert Disagreement, something is objective if and only if it is the product and the result of (i.e., survives) the most intense debate between the most disparate points of view that we can arrange on an important topic.

And finally, in Systems Thinking, something is objective if and only if it is the product and the result of the most intense effort of sweeping in different knowledge from the arts, humanities, professions, philosophy, sciences, etc.

What then does it mean to be "objective?" To be "objective" is to "choose" the "'appropriate' mode of inquiry depending upon the purposes of one's study." And, to "choose" means to debate which mode of inquiry is "best" in light of knowledge of all the various modes.

Finally, the philosophical school of Pragmatism disputes the whole distinction between objectivity and subjectivity altogether. Indeed, Pragmatism disputes all timeworn and outmoded dualisms such as the mind versus the body, subjective versus objective, hard versus soft, etc. Given that all knowledge is the product of human inquiry, there is a "human subject" behind every determination of the "facts," and "truth," if not "reality itself."

The Problem with Education

Traditional education and science primarily stress only the first two ways of knowing or systems of inquiry: Expert Agreement and the One Best or True Formula. Educators pound "well-accepted facts" based on the first way of knowing, Expert Agreement, into our heads, and they stress knowledge of "well-accepted theories"—The One Best

Formula—in solving problems. Anything that cannot be reduced to hard data, facts, or observations—the first way–or represented in terms of accepted theories–the second way—is false, dangerous, and misleading.

The first and the second ways are historically the foundations of education and of knowledge for a traditional "round world," i.e., countries and regions that are separated by clear geographic boundaries, time zones, national identities, and distinct economies. But they are seriously deficient and inadequate for a "flat world," i.e., metaphorically speaking, a world that is globally and increasingly interconnected along every conceivable dimension, in short, a world that is composed of complex, messy problems from top to bottom. First of all, the first and the second ways are too restrictive. They assume that the problems we need to solve are already well known and well defined. But as I have stressed throughout, the "problem" with most problems is "to define what the problems are in the first place."

The first two ways are not well suited for complex problems such as the 2008 financial crisis. The definition, let alone the resolution, of the financial crisis (especially the avoidance of future such crises) is as difficult and as messy as defeating ISIS. This is precisely where the third (Multiple Formulas), the fourth (Expert Disagreement), and the fifth (Systems Thinking) ways are required.

The third way, Multiple Formulas or Perspectives, says that we explicitly need to see multiple definitions of a problem so that we can attempt to avoid Type Three Errors. How can we even begin to assess, let alone know, if we are "solving the 'wrong problems' precisely" if we don't have more than one formulation of a problem for our explicit consideration? We can't.

Once again, comparing two or more different formulations of a problem is no iron-glad guarantee that we will solve the right problems. At best, it is a minimal guarantor. But, we can say that without examining explicitly two or more different formulations of a problem, the probability of committing Type Three Errors goes up considerably.

The third, fourth, and fifth ways require us to exercise judgment, and an even more precious commodity, wisdom.

The Moral

The moral of the story is <u>not</u> that we should never use the first two ways of knowing, but that we should use them only after we have assured ourselves that, by using the third, fourth, and fifth ways, we are working on the "right problems" to begin with. The third, fourth, and fifth ways are best suited for problem formulation; in contrast, the first two ways are best suited for problem solving, once we have assured ourselves that we have defined the "right problems."

A complex, globally interconnected world requires that we "manage" complex, messy problems not solve them exactly them as we attempted to do in a simpler, fragmented world. A complex, globally interconnected world also requires that we acknowledge that the predominant philosophical bases of a simpler, fragmented world—the first two ways of knowing—do not apply in their entirety. They apply only in the sense that we still collect data when we can and we still apply accepted scientific thinking, but we accept their limitations.

In the end, one of the most essential aspects of Systems Thinking is the realization that we only get out of inquiry what we put into it initially. And, what we fundamentally put into every inquiry is ourselves through our collective psychology.

In far too many cases, we are obsessed with what John Dewey referred to as <u>The Quest for Certainty</u>.[11] The first two ways differ only in where they locate the certainty we so desperately seek. The first way, Expert Agreement, attempts to find certainty in hard data and Expert Consensus, supposedly the "facts" on which everyone can agree. The second way, The One Best Formula, attempts to find it in the "indisputable scientific laws of nature, pure thought, or abstract logic." For Dewey, both were neurotic attempts on the part of humankind to manage the anxiety brought about by a dangerous and uncertain world into which all of us are born. Notice carefully that Dewey did not say that "basic facts" or "elemental truths" were neurotic in themselves. What was neurotic was our obsessive need for certainty.

The danger is not that we will agree, but that we will agree too readily by being pressured to go along with crowd.

Fake News, the Product of Fake Inquiry

As Jonathan Mahler has observed:

> ...In the age of Trump, you don't need to act to create your own reality; you can just tweet, whether it's bogus crime and unemployment statistics or made-up accusations of widespread voter fraud...In a world with no universally standards for truth—a world in which journalists engaged in the study of discernible reality are dismissed as 'dishonest' and 'corrupt—everything is fair game...[12]

The concept of Inquiry Systems is one of the most powerful ways of which I know for analyzing the phenomenon of Fake News. In brief, Fake News is the product of Fake Inquiry, the perverse use of Inquiry Systems for perverse ends.

Those who are susceptible to Fake News—especially to various forms of conspiracy theories—generally start with a set of "preconceived truths"—for example, "one can't trust the national news media because they are irredeemably biased against conservative views, etc." (We all start with preconceived truths of some sort so by itself this is not especially damning. It's the inability to give up our beliefs in the face of strong counter evidence in the form of Rebuttals that is disconcerting.) These "truths" are so strongly held that they are irrefutable. One then works backwards to find sources (data, Evidence, spokespersons, etc.) that unequivocally support one's predetermined views. Instead of using independent, well-qualified journalists who are experts in seeking out facts and counterchecking them meticulously, in its place, one gravitates toward a group of partisan advocates with whom one agrees instinctively. These are one's "'true' experts."

Well-known cognitive biases are paramount in both forming and confirming one's favored beliefs. Thus, confirmation bias—deliberately searching out those sources that support one's favored conclusions—is predominant. So is cognitive closure. One's preferred truths are impervious to modification.

Unfortunately, with the growth of social media, one cannot counter Fake News merely by presenting scientific evidence and lucid reasoning alone (ST, NT). One needs friendly faces that can embed scientific evidence and reasoning in compelling stories (NF, SF).

If social media were truly responsible, then long before it was pressured to do so, it would have already developed means that were devoted exclusively to countering Fake News. It would have employed social scientists and other valid experts to test what's most effective in counteracting Fake News. It was only after the hue and cry was so loud and persistent such that it couldn't be ignored any longer that Facebook finally hired an independent organization to help filter out Fake News.

The point is that we're greatly mistaken if not naive if we think that "scientific facts" alone will counter Fake News. It wouldn't exist if it didn't fulfill deep emotional needs. Without understanding the depths of such needs, we are powerless to counteract them.

One of the most important aspects of Fake News has to do with Expert Disagreement. Ideally, both sides of a dialectic should be equally credible. Sadly, such is not always the case. Ideally, liberals try to use credible sources and impartial evidence to dispute Fake News. Conservatives often label Fake anything that does not agree with their ideology.[13] But then, so do liberals.

Notes

1. Jonathan Mahler, "Search Party," *The Sunday New York Times Magazine*, January 1, 2017, p. 10.
2. Tom Nichols, "How America Lost Faith in Expertise," *Foreign Affairs*, March/April, 2017, p. 61.
3. Ian. I. Mitroff, The *Unbounded Mind: Breaking the Chains of Traditional Business Thinking*, Oxford University Press, New York, 1993.
4. Mitroff and Silvers, op. cit.
5. An Inquiry System consists of: Inputs, an Operator that transforms the Inputs into Outputs, which are then regarded as the "truth." One of the most critical features of an Inquiry System is what Churchman labels the "guarantor." The guarantor is that feature of an inquiry system that "guarantees" that if one starts with the "right kind of Inputs," operates on them in the "right way," then the Output(s) of the

system will be the "truth." In the first model, the tighter the agreement between experts, i.e., the stronger the agreement between them, supposedly the "more" that the agreement is or approaches the truth. Thus, in the first model, the guarantor is the agreement between independent experts. Notice that the guarantor and the operator are confounded. That is, they are not independent. Agreement is the operator—it is used to manufacture or to produce the output—and agreement is also the guarantor of the system as well. For this reason, one is well advised to be suspicious of how agreement is obtained, e.g., whether it is forced or not.

6. There is nothing wrong per se in using one method initially to select another method of reaching an important decision. Once we have all of the various methods at our disposal, we can use them in various combinations. The important point is the pure methods, systems, or models themselves are rarely discussed in the arena of business, let alone their combinations.

7. See the previous footnote.

8. Quoted in David Marcum and Steven Smith, *Egonomics*, Simon and Schuster, New York, 2007, 132.

9. See C. West Churchman, *The Design of Inquiring Systems*, Basic Books, 1971.

10. Ian I. Mitroff, *The Subjective Side of Science: A Philosophical Investigation into the Psychology of the Apollo Moon Scientists*, Elsevier, Amsterdam, 1974.

11. John Dewey, *The Quest for Certainty*, Putnam, New York, 1960.

12. Mahler, op. cit., p. 11.

13. Jeremy W. Peter, "Wielding Claims of 'Fake News,' Conservatives Take Aim at Mainstream Media," *The New York Times*, Monday, December 26, 2016, p. A11.

13

Future Crises, William James, John Dewey, Edward Singer, C. West Churchman

In my home office, I have a photostatic copy of a 1896 letter from William James, arguably one of America's and the world's greatest philosophers, to the provost of The University of Pennsylvania. In his letter, James recommends Edward Singer Jr. for a position in philosophy at Penn. James states that in his 30 years of giving instruction in philosophy, Singer is the best all around student he has had. There was no branch of philosophy that Singer hadn't mastered and thus couldn't teach well.

Singer went on to have a long and distinguished career at Penn. One of his most successful students, C. West Churchman, was the person who later taught me philosophy. Thus, if intellectually speaking Singer is my grandfather, then William James is intellectually my great-grandfather, a fact of which I couldn't be more proud.

Although he didn't use it for thinking about future crises, one of Singer's greatest contributions provides an important way of approaching the issue. Obviously, no one knows for sure what future opportunities, let alone crises, will exactly be, but for this reason, we need to broaden our thinking as much as possible.

© The Author(s) 2019
I. I. Mitroff, *Technology Run Amok*,
https://doi.org/10.1007/978-3-319-95741-8_13

129

Positivism

Singer lived and wrote at the time when the philosophy of Positivism was in its heyday. Positivism posited that logic, mathematics, and physics were the basic fields of knowledge to which all propositions needed to be subject to—better yet, "reduced to"—before any Claim was accepted as true. Before any contention was accepted, it had to be either a logically true statement such as "Every person is either six feet tall or is not six feet tall." It's thus logically impossible that anyone can be both 6 feet and 7 feet tall at the same time. Or, it had to be a statement that was true because it could be verified empirically by direct observation. Anything else was pure speculation.

No wonder why the Positivists were contemptuous in their rejection of metaphysics, which to them was nothing more than unprovable, meaningless conjectures, for example, whether God existed or not. Of course, Positivism was later discredited because it merely substituted its own special brand of metaphysics in discrediting others. Namely, why was the essence of anything known only by logic and empiricism alone? That's an unproven generalization if ever there was one! In other words, the basic tenets of Positivism didn't meet—indeed, couldn't meet—its own severe standards.

Furthermore, according to Positivism, the "hard sciences" such as logic, math, and physics were at the top of the heap of knowledge and the social sciences, history, philosophy, the humanities in general were at the bottom. Logic came first because every science in its desire to reach firm conclusions had to presuppose the science of logic, i.e., "correct reasoning." Mathematics and the physical sciences followed closely because they offered the promise of "hard knowledge about the physical world." The social sciences, history, philosophy, the humanities in general were at the bottom because they did not meet the high standards for attaining knowledge that supposedly the hard sciences did. They were too "soft" in that they were filled with unproved speculations. It thus comes as no surprise that psychoanalytic thinking was regarded as among the very worst. It was little better than theology, if that.

Once again, Pragmatism rejects in the strongest possible terms the vulgar distinction between "hard" and "soft" branches of knowledge.

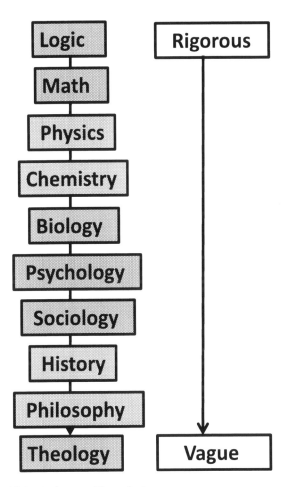

Fig. 13.1 Positivism's theory of knowledge

According to Positivism, the various fields of knowledge—if all of them could even be accorded the status of "knowledge"—could therefore be arrayed in a strict linear hierarchy depending on how rigorous they were and on how much other fields presupposed them. Thus, all fields presupposed logic since once again they are all dependent on reaching valid conclusions, but pure logic didn't presuppose anything else other than pure thought itself. Figure 13.1 is a representation of Positivistic thought.

Challenging Positivism

Singer challenged Positivism head on at its very core. He showed that all of the sciences and fields of knowledge were on an even par. Every science and field of knowledge presupposed all of the others in order to do its job, if not for its basic existence. To demonstrate this, Singer took a seemingly simple example and showed that it was far more complex than how Positivism conceived of it.

Since early in his career Singer was a civil engineer, he took the supposedly simple, if not trivial, example of measuring the distance between two points A and B. According to the Positivists, one merely took a ruler or a measuring tape and just read off the single, exact number representing the true distance. For Singer, this was a gross misrepresentation of what measurement entailed. For one, the Positivists assumed that a ruler and measuring tape were already properly calibrated so that the measurements were automatically correct. But calibration is never to be taken-for-granted, especially if the measurements are important. That is, how do we know that a measuring instrument is giving correct readings?

For another, suppose as was typically the case that the distance between A and B was such that it crossed a number of city blocks, counties, and even state lines. Then, the profession of law would automatically be involved in ensuring that proper legal procedures were followed and property rights were respected. Since teams of people would necessarily be required to take and to verify the measurements, psychology and sociology would also automatically be involved in helping to ensure that there were the proper kinds of cooperation between groups of people and that biases were accounted for.

Even if the distance was short, it still wasn't necessarily a simple problem. Suppose that a great deal was riding on the outcome, say whether a wall was or was not a part of one's property, then the measurements would need to be repeated to see if they clustered around a central number. Thus, the science of statistics would invariably be involved.

In this way, Singer showed that all of the various sciences and professions presupposed all of the others in doing their basic jobs. Thus, where the Positivists proposed a linear hierarchical model of knowledge,

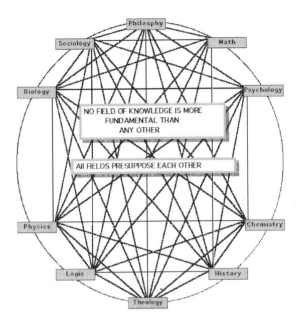

Fig. 13.2 Singer's view of knowledge

Singer proposed in essence a circular wheel-like model shown below in Fig. 13.2.

In Fig. 13.2, the lines between the various fields represent what each contributes to the others so that it can perform its basic functions. Thus, the science of psychology contributes to physics in the sense that physics is done by complex humans that are subject to innumerable biases and limitations that not only affect what they see in the first place, but how they interpret it subsequently. For ease of presentation, all of the various sciences and professions are not shown as part of Fig. 13.2, but they are there in principle.

Novel Alignments

Now that we have Fig. 13.2, we can use it in ways that Singer didn't envision, but for which I have no doubt whatsoever that if he were alive today, he would. Since chips, implants, and the use of robots are already underway, we need not dwell on how physics—and technology in general—and medicine are reshaping one another. In the same way, we need not dwell on the alignment between psychology and computer science when it comes to Artificial Intelligence. These fields are already well underway.

The real use of Fig. 13.2 is with regard to those fields whose alignment we don't normally imagine. Thus, theology and business came together in the field of spirituality at work, of which I was one of the early contributors.[1]

One of the most important uses of Fig. 13.2 is looking for early warning signals that not only announce the creation of new fields, but whether they will lead to positive opportunities versus major crises.

Concluding Remarks

The purpose of this chapter has been to offer a broad way of thinking about the potential interactions between any and all of the various sciences and professions. In this regard, Fig. 13.2 is a template. It's certainly not predictive, for no one can envisage with perfect certainty what the future will be like. One thing however I feel certain about. The most improbable matches will occur.

Notice that it applies to looking at how various technologies affect one another.

Finally, the chapter reveals one of the most important characteristic features of Systems Thinking. The various science and professions are interdependent, not independent. No wonder why I was drawn so strongly to the ideas of James, Singer, Churchman, and Ackoff.

Note

1. Ian I. Mitroff and Elizabeth Denton, *A Spiritual Audit od Corporate America: A Hard Look at Spirituality, Religion, and Values*, Jossey-Bass, San Francisco, CA, 1999.

14

Epilogue

Natasha Singer provides a fitting note on which to end:

> Unlike Apple or Microsoft, which make money primarily by selling devices or software services, Google derives most of its revenue from online advertising—much of it targeted through sophisticated use of people's data. Questions about how Google might use data gleaned from students' online activities have dogged the company for years.
>
> 'Unless we know what is collected, why it is collected, how it is used and a review of it is possible, we can never understand with certainty how this information could be used to help or hurt a kid,' said Bill Fitzgerald of Common Sense Media, a children's advocacy group, who vets the security and privacy of classroom apps.[1]

I come back to one of the prime concerns with which I started: All of the marvelous gadgets that we are madly inventing are not only greatly transforming the external world around us, but even more, they are greatly revolutionizing us as well—emotionally, physically, and socially to the very depths of our being. They are reinventing us as much, if not more, than we are inventing them. As such, they offer unparalleled opportunities as well as the potential for horrific crises.

© The Author(s) 2019
I. I. Mitroff, *Technology Run Amok*,
https://doi.org/10.1007/978-3-319-95741-8_14

To make matters worse, as the quote above is testimony, tech companies have not, to put it mildly, always behaved responsibility. To the contrary, they have generally fought tooth and nail reasonable regulations. For this and other reasons, there have been repeated calls to reconstitute them as media companies where they could be better supervised and regulated. I couldn't agree more.

One of the very few tech persons to take responsibility for his invention is Evan Williams, the founder of Twitter. In a recent *New York Times* article, Mr. Williams is quoted as saying that the Internet is broken:

'I thought once everybody could speak freely and exchange information and ideas, the world is automatically going to be a better place,' Mr. Williams says. 'I was wrong about that.'[2]

As David Streitfeld, the author of the article about Mr. Williams, put it:

People are using Facebook to showcase suicides, beatings, and murder, in real time. Twitter is hive of tolling and abuse that it seems unable to stop. Fake news, whether created for ideology or profit, runs rampant. Four out of 10 adults said …that they had been harassed online. And that was before the presidential campaign heated up last year.[3]

A Deficit of Empathy

In her latest book, <u>Reclaiming Conversation: The Power of Talk in a Digital Age</u>,[4] Sherry Turkle recounts the many talks she has had with elementary school teachers. Sadly, the teachers noted time and again that young children enter school with a profound deficiency in their ability to show empathy toward others. All of the considerable amounts of time they have spent on iPads and iPhones has lessened their ability to relate to others in meaningful ways.

In this regard, it's highly instructive to compare the language used by Professor Turkle with that Pascale Fung, a professor of electronic and computer engineering. Professor Fung and her colleagues are busily engaged in creating "Robots With Heart."[5] To do this, they are creating "Empathy Modules," i.e., orchestrated sets of rules that mimic empathy. The contrast between Professor Turkle (NF, SF) and Professor Fung (ST, NT) couldn't be clearer. Talk about a deficit!

The Inversion the Moral Responsibility Principles

The complex, messy systems we've created are messing with us in ways we've not foreseen largely because we've been mesmerized by our marvelous creations. We've been overly enticed by their positive virtues. Little wonder why it's so difficult to think about their downsides. Much of this is due to our Splitting the world into "good" versus "bad guys, forces, etc.," and focusing primarily on the "good." As a result, in attempting to cope with complex, messy systems, one must always be on the lookout for the ruinous effects of Splitting.

Bar none, one of the hardest tasks facing humankind is thinking systematically about how all of the positive attributes and virtues of our marvelous inventions can turn into their direct opposites and thus become harmful. Who likes to think about the fact that what one has created with the best of intentions can become an agent of harm, and worst of all, evil? This is precisely why one needs special methods and procedures that will allow and encourage one to consider the downsides of one's creations. It needs to be as deliberate and systematic as the initial processes of invention.

The fact that positives can easily turn into negatives I call The Inversion Principle. Taking responsibility for negative impacts is the Moral Responsibility Principle. The following demonstrates how one can indeed think about the unthinkable.

Thinking the Unthinkable: The Internal Assassin Team

Many years ago, I visited a major pharmaceutical company in the hopes of learning what they were doing to combat a chief potential crisis that was always lurking in the shadows, product tampering. When I asked the person who agreed to talk to me about what they were doing, without losing a beat, he said, "We formed two Internal Assassin Teams." To which, I blurted out, "You did what?!"

The person went on to say. "One day we held up one of the bottles of our painkillers and we looked at the cap as the front door of a house and the sides as the walls. We then asked ourselves, 'How could a burglar get in, remain undetected for as long as possible, and thereby do the most damage?' Since we knew more about our products and production systems than anybody else, that's when we got the idea of putting together two Internal Assassin Teams to see if they could come up with creative ways to attack our products. One team was composed of people with only a high-school education and the other with advanced graduate degrees. We soon learned that there was no way to keep a determined burglar out so that the idea of tamper-proof bottles was not even a remote possibility. Finally, we hit on tamper-evident seals. That was the best that anyone could do."

Notice the creativity involved (NT, NF). It's not with inventing a new product or idea. It's with how to protect an already invented product by doing everything possible to attack and destroy it! I seriously doubt that any Artificial Intelligence (AI) program or scheme could come up with the idea of Internal Assassin teams and then apply it to one's products. But then this is precisely why crisis management requires continual creativity. It's not just a matter of computing the probabilities and consequences of potential risks and crises. It demands constant creativity.

General Psychology

Much of our inability to think about the downsides of our inventions is also due to general psychology. Technology is predominantly a young person's game. Unfortunately, males also dominate it. In short, they are in a state of "arrested development." That is, while they look like adults, they are emotionally undeveloped.

Most people don't mature until they are well into their twenties and even thirties. This means that they are largely unable to envision the ethical and social impacts of their work until then. But this means that adults whether in the form of funders or the government have to step in and monitor the creations of younger minds. In other words, those who are the inventors of a technology or business are not always the best ones to manage it. The skills that are involved in inventing and creating a new technology (ST, NT) are not the skills that are required for managing it (NF, SF).

As we've seen, in coping with wicked messes, what's presumed to be "good" has an uncanny way of turning into something that's decidedly "bad." That's precisely why in terms of Inquiry Systems, Dialectical Thinking is an absolute requirement. In addition, one must also be cognizant of paradoxes such as More Lead to Less, etc. Again, this calls for more than a modicum of maturity.

In sum, coping with complex, messy systems—wicked messes—calls for a major transformation/revolution in our thinking, not to mention in all of our leading institutions as well.

Redesigning Universities

Finally, the concept of wicked messes leads to ideas for the fundamental redesign of universities. At their best, all university departments—certainly the humanities and social sciences—have been working on parts of various messes: homelessness, income inequality, reform of the penal system, the redesign of K-12 and higher education, etc. What has not been done is to make wicked messes the centerpiece of every department and program in universities. For instance, given their importance, the time is way overdue the establishment of Journals for Wicked Messes! If they existed and were given the status they deserve, professors would then be promoted based on their work on adding to our knowledge of wicked messes, for example, in furthering our knowledge of heuristics for coping with them, not to mention specific ideas for actually implementing ways of managing specific messes.

The notion of faculty, at the very least faculty participation, also needs to be broadened. Those who experience the full impact of wicked messes need to have a fundamental say with regard to which messes are chosen for investigation, and how they are investigated. They certainly need to be involved in every step of the investigations.

And, "publication" needs to be fundamentally rethought. I would argue that publication of one's results in <u>The Huffington Post</u> or any major newspaper that reaches a wide audience is as important as any journal article or paper.

Concluding Remarks

The technology community has created enormous crises for itself. By generally being unable and unwilling to get out in front of them before they happen, it's set itself up for direct government oversight and intervention. As I've noted, such efforts are already underway in the UK. Legislation has already been passed that will protect children from the worst excesses of technology.

It bears repeating: Those who have the technical knowledge and competence (ST, NT) to invent the marvelous technologies that are integral parts of our lives do not necessarily have the accompanying social, managerial knowledge, and skills (NF, SF)—in short, the maturity—that are necessary to manage their marvelous creations. They are so mesmerized by the positive aspects of their inventions that they are virtually unable to consider the inevitable negative aspects, let alone to do anything serious about them until the worst actually happens. They offer little but the flimsiest of excuses why they couldn't have done anything better in anticipating horrible situations such as videos showing the execution of innocent victims.

The technology community has only itself to blame for not practicing proactive crisis management. While not perfect by any means, proactive crisis management is the best we have in anticipating and planning for the worst, and especially, doing everything humanely possible to ensure that it never happens. But to do this requires technology companies with a greater conscience. Designing and sustaining ethical technology companies are a task of the utmost importance. Nothing less ensures that technology will continue to be one of the greatest threats facing humankind.

Notes

1. Natasha Singer, "How Google Conquered the American Classroom, Schools Transformed by Tech Giant May Be Giving More Than They're Getting," *The New York Times*, Sunday, May 14, 2017, p. 18.
2. David Streitfeld, "The Internet Is Broken," *The New York Times*, Sunday, May 24, 2017, p. BU 1.
3. Ibid.
4. Sherry Turkle, *Reclaiming Conversation: The Power of Talk in a Digital Age*, Penguin, New York, 2015.
5. Pascale Funf, "Robots with Heart," *Scientific American*, November 2015, pp. 61–63.

Index

© The Editor(s) (if applicable) and The Author(s), under exclusive licence
to Springer International Publishing AG, part of Springer Nature 2019
I. I. Mitroff, *Technology Run Amok*, https://doi.org/10.1007/978-3-319-95741-8

Printed in the United States
By Bookmasters